A *Homecoming* CHRISTMAS

Presented to

_____

BY

_____

ON

_____

BILL & GLORIA GAITHER

A

Homecoming

CHRISTMAS

*Sensing the
Wonders of
the Season*

WORTHY
PUBLISHING

Published by Worthy Publishing, a division of Worthy Media, Inc.,
134 Franklin Road, Suite 200, Brentwood, Tennessee 37027.

HELPING PEOPLE EXPERIENCE THE HEART OF GOD

eBook available at www.worthypublishing.com

Audio distributed through Oasis Audio; visit www.oasisaudio.com

Library of Congress Control Number: 2011936269

For foreign and subsidiary rights, contact Riggins International Rights Services, Inc.; www.rigginsrights.com

ISBN: 978-1-936034-51-2 (hardcover w/ jacket)

Cover Design: Christopher Tobias

Cover Photos: tree - ©Jim Craigmyle/Corbis; Bill and Gloria Gaither – in winter coats: ©Tammy Blevins; with gift and greenery: ©Nancy Bailey Pratt; headshots above biography information: ©Nancy Bailey Pratt

Interior Design and Typesetting: Roy Roper, wideyedesign

Printed in the United States of America
11 12 13 14 15 16 17 LBM 8 7 6 5 4 3 2 1

TABLE OF Contents

A *Homecoming* CHRISTMAS

II. The Sounds of Christmas

III. Touching Christmas

IV. The Fragrance of Christmas

Sensing

The Mystery of Christmas

I like to think of the mind
as the center city
into which flows
five major highways:
sight, sound, smell,
touch, and taste.
It is by way of
these thoroughfares
that we experience life
in all of its complexity.

It is by the senses that we learn, gain insights, and internalize all that is true and helpful for life.

If ever there were a truth that needed to be internalized in every way, it is the amazing story of a God who spoke all things into existence and continues to sustain creation with His breath, yet who loved His creation so much that He Himself came as a helpless baby to touch us at our point of need. When we weren't understanding the immensity of His love for His creation, He spoke His love in terms we could comprehend: the sound of a baby's cry on a cold night, the smell of a lowly, animal-filled stable, the rough texture of a feeding trough filled with coarse straw, the brightness of a new star in the dark night sky, and the taste of the Bread of Life to feed the souls of us all.

Since that night more than two millennia ago that divided time itself into B.C. (before) and A.D. (after), those whose lives have been changed by this baby boy have created dozens of symbols and traditions in their efforts to express an event both human and divine. All the senses have been called into play by the deep longing to share the very personal experiences of a cosmic and eternal change-point.

Light, warmth, belonging, satisfaction of deep unnameable hungers, fresh and eternal life, spiritual pilgrimage, the divine gifts, the return of the Song of Life . . . all these need the ladder of symbol to even begin to approach and express the depths of Redeeming Love!

Each of us has been the recipient of a rich heritage of traditions and symbols given by others so that we can experience and communicate to our children the unfathomable love of God. The God who came to walk with us, to touch us where we are broken, to feed us the true water and food of the Spirit, and to be His love made visible.

As we celebrate Christmas, let's use all the senses—every avenue we have—to embrace this amazing Story. And as we do, let's remember to always tell and retell the *reason* for every tradition, giving thanks for the *reality* we celebrate! Let's promise each other that every highway to the soul will never become a bypass.

Gloria Gaither

WORSHIPING WITH ALL *Our Senses*
~ *Calvin Miller* ~

They say it never snows in Bethlehem!
Too bad for little Jesus! He never saw it snow.
I wish His infant eyes had seen
this ice-bright land.
For snow can sanctify a holy night
With jeweled elegance and formal white.

CALVIN MILLER
"THEY SAY IT NEVER SNOWS IN BETHLEHEM"

Wonder is the holy hush we feel

when we contemplate the season of His birth.

And feeling Christmas is the only way

we ever can fully measure the awe

that is born in us each December.

Those of us who love the Savior

love equally the celebration of His birth.

Our souls in such a season

magnify the Lord so greatly

that nothing can ever dampen

the fullness of our joy.

Christmas comes to us singular and entire.

Can we divide the wonder? Into what?

The sacred and the secular?

Continued on page 6

My most precious gift was a mother and father who constantly and consistently taught me what was important in life. This is a piece my mother wrote for a magazine in which she authored a column. Her wisdom still speaks to us, our children, and their children.

GLORIA GAITHER

DOROTHY SICKAL
Let Bygones Be Remembered

If I could tell every parent something to enrich their children's memories of Christmas, I would share three things:

1. Forget the commercial idea that you must spend the same amount of money for each child. It is not a good way to teach children to deny self by giving one's best to others. Their needs cannot be the same, so why draw attention to the dollars spent? I have actually seen people try to add up the commercial value of their "loot."

2. Material gifts are poor collateral for love. Never try to redeem poor parenting, meanness, unfairness, inconsistency, or immorality with lavish gifts. When they get this figured out, they will think less of you instead of more.

3. Let the gifts be an expression of forgiveness, of joy, giving because your children are loved—and never with a you-have-to-earn-this attitude. This is a "give like Jesus" season.

Hope that children will treasure and take care of a gift. Trashing things given in love will shame the recipient sooner or later; at least, it should.

Responsibility goes with every gift from God or others.

My most precious Christmas memory: after my parents left their South Dakota ranch, they moved to the Missouri Ozarks with all their possessions and five children in a covered wagon. It was late autumn when we moved into the tiny house. My father had bought a rocky stump farm from an ad he saw in the *Missouri Farmer*. It was at a time when nearly every man wanted to move west—or somewhere other than where he was—and every woman was taught that, regardless of wisdom, family needs, or hardship, she must go along. We never thought about keeping up with the Joneses; we seldom stayed in one place long enough to know the Joneses.

Mama spared no labor to make our Christmas special. Many times it took much inventive effort and long hours under the feeble glow of the oil lamp after the children were asleep. Papa helped in every way he could and, although he was not a good carpenter, he used hammer and saw to fashion some new toy mother dreamed up. If it came short of her expectations, she worked it over to perfection. A little paint covered a multitude of sins.

They never gave us a guilt-trip by lamenting how much work it was or belaboring their poverty. My parents were both very energetic, and I always felt that they enjoyed what they did. They never seemed to measure what we

> MAMA SPARED
> NO LABOR TO MAKE
> OUR CHRISTMAS SPECIAL...
> PAPA HELPED
> IN EVERY WAY HE COULD

had by what others had. They believed that laziness and ignorance were the shame of the universe. They would have been horrified at the idea of taking a government hand-out.

My little brother, Roy, and I were four and eight years old. And we had a hard time believing in Santa Claus. We decided to go along with it, like fairies and elves, to please Mama. Roy said, "How could some old man at the North Pole know where we live?" It just didn't make sense. Mama used the word, but it sounded phony to us.

On this particular Christmas morning, I was unprepared for the wonder of it all. A heavy frost made ferns and rivers on the thin windowpanes. Old Frank's breath sent up great puffs of frosty steam as he barked on the porch. The trees cracked and popped when the wind swayed their branches. It was like Sunday, only different. The fire in the front-room stove glowed red and warm when we rushed inside to look at the little tree by the window.

Then I saw a beautiful red rocking chair on which sat an elegant doll. I barely noticed that the chair was the little oak rocker I had gotten in South Dakota. And the doll, with her wavy black, painted hair and her snow-white face with its bright red cheeks, had a whole new body. She wore a fluffy white dress with lace and ribbons. Her petticoats and panties were edged with lace. Her oil-cloth black patent shoes were over white-ribbed stockings. I think she was made dearer because I had already known her and loved her. It was pure magic.

For Roy there was a stick horse, painted shiny white with a leather bridle and reins. His head was black fur and his eyes were big white buttons with black pupils. Two little wheels were fastened to the end of the stick, and they rolled merrily along when Roy galloped around the kitchen table.

There was a hickory bow and arrow for my brother Rollie, and a jumping jack. Daddy was a good whittler.

There were brown paper bags for each family member with an orange in every one—an orange we could eat all by ourselves. There were peanuts in the shells, and a popcorn ball. Who could ask for more?

Hot biscuits and gravy, eggs and bacon steamed on the breakfast table. Mama's red jelly sparkled in its jars.

There were no plastic toys we could have played with in the stores before Christmas until they seemed dull. There was no fighting and arguing as we plowed through yards of paper and ribbons. And a whole day to play and stare at the magic around us.

What does it really take to make a good Christmas? ❊

A big orange and some fresh pine boughs
and "Silent Night" are all I need,
and cookies, of course.
They are the strings that when I pull on them
I pull up the complete glittering
storybook Christmases of my childhood.

GARRISON KEILLOR

THE SYMBOLS
of Christmas

The God of the universe has
"moved into the neighborhood!"
God is with us! Emmanuel!
Let's make sure our children understand each symbol:
the star, the lights, the green of new life,
the red of blood, the angels, the priceless gifts,
the shepherds and sheep,
the lowly stable and manger.
Tell the story with every tree, centerpiece, mantle,
tradition, and with special food.
Keep the meaning of every gift and every song!

BILL & GLORIA GAITHER

CHRISTMAS COLORS

Over the years, the traditional Christmas colors—red, green, and white—have been used to signify the Christmas story. Green, to represent eternal life; red, to remind us of the blood that Christ would shed for our sins; white, to signify the purity our hearts can find only through His forgiveness. Often we see accents of gold to represent the costly offering brought to Him by the wise men, or silver that has been refined just as we are refined through our faith and obedience to the Savior.

The well-known Christmas carol "The Holly and the Ivy" reaches back in origin more than a thousand years. But not until it was published by Cecil Sharp did people discover how this old favorite explains so beautifully the colors we associate with Christmas as represented in the ivy and holly with which we deck our halls! ❊

Karen Peck-Gooch dresses her tree in red, green, and gold . . . all colors that remind us of the life, sacrifice, and majesty of Christ.

The Holly and The Ivy

WRITER UNKNOWN

The holly and the ivy,
When they are both full grown,
Of all the trees that are in the wood
The holly bears the crown.

The holly bears a blossom
As white as lily flower;
And Mary bore sweet Jesus Christ
To be our sweet Saviour.

The holly bears a berry
As red as any blood;
And Mary bore sweet Jesus Christ
To do poor sinners good.

The holly bears a prickle
As sharp as any thorn;
And Mary bore sweet Jesus Christ
On Christmas Day in the morn.

The holly bears a bark
As bitter as any gall;
And Mary bore sweet Jesus Christ
For to redeem us all.

The holly and the ivy,
now both are full well grown,
Of all the trees that are in the wood
The holly bears the crown.

O the rising of the sun
And the running of the deer
The playing of the merry organ
Sweet singing of the choir

Worshiping
WITH ALL OUR SENSES
~ Calvin Miller ~

Some of Christmas—
most of it—is secular, they say.
It is the stuff of a winter festival.
There are elves and reindeer
and peppermints and snowmen.
And some of it—
the least of it, some say—is sacred:
the descent of God into human flesh.
It is the baffling mystery of a Jewish baby born
for His own execution and our redemption.
The sacred and secular motifs
in time were bound to be spun
into a single entanglement.
There is the general feeling
that we need to keep Santa and Jesus
in separate pockets all through Christmas.
The shepherds and elves simply pass too close.
Angels and sleigh rides are odd companions.
Which of the tales is about the North Pole and
which is about Bethlehem?
Which of the motifs contain camels,
and which reindeer?
Which holds the fictions of
the Grinch who stole Christmas,
and which holds the story of
the infant-killing Herod?

Continued on page 11

THE CHRISTMAS TREE

The Christmas tree, however simple or elaborate, stands as a timeless testament to all that Christmas means, to all that is joyful and holy about the celebration of Jesus' birth.

Evergreen symbolizes the eternal life Christ was born to give us. The branches bear reminders of the beauty, joy, and hope of this season. Lights illuminate even the darkest corners with sweet light. The top—the focal point—glows with a reminder of the guiding star and angelic choir that announced His arrival. ❋

O Christmas tree, O Christmas tree,
How lovely are your branches!
In beauty green will always grow
Through summer sun and winter snow.
O Christmas tree, O Christmas tree,
How lovely are your branches!

O Christmas tree, O Christmas tree,
You are the tree most loved!
How often you give us delight
In brightly shining Christmas light!
O Christmas tree, O Christmas tree,
You are the tree most loved!

O Christmas tree, O Christmas tree,
Your beauty green will teach me
That hope and love will ever be
The way to joy and peace for me.
O Christmas tree, O Christmas tree,
Your beauty green will teach me.

WRITER UNKNOWN
"O CHRISTMAS TREE"

From our homes to heavily traveled places like the Opryland Hotel in Nashville, Tennessee, the Christmas tree (left, shot by Lori Phelps) stands as a radiant image, drawing our attention to the story of Christmas. From the simplest to the most elaborate, Nativities (like this one, right, that Solveig Leithaug displays in her Nashville home) tell the Story without a single spoken word.

THE NATIVITY

Be near me, Lord Jesus,
I ask Thee to stay
Close by me forever
And love me I pray

WRITER UNKNOWN
"AWAY IN A MANGER"
Music composed by William J. Kirkpatrick

Who has not been moved a little closer to the Story by seeing that manger at the center of the Nativity scene, holding the Savior of the world? Who hasn't lingered at the sight of His mother seated in the hay by His side with the young carpenter, worshiping this baby King whom they would raise? Who hasn't imagined the initial terror—then the unmitigated joy—of the shepherds when the angels burst onto their quiet hillside with trumpets and songs announcing the birth of the Messiah? And the wise men bearing lavish gifts, traveling mile after uncomfortable mile to see the infant for themselves and to express their

worship? Every reminder of this incredible story brings its reality closer. This is not a manufactured legend men have spun and embellished over the centuries. It is real!

Somehow this scene—whether on a Christmas card, placed as a reminder at home, or reenacted by humans—always touches us more deeply than simply imagining it in our minds. ❄

THE STAR

O star of wonder, star of light
Star with royal beauty bright
Westward leading, still proceeding
Guide us to thy perfect light.

REV. JOHN HENRY HOPKINS
"WE THREE KINGS"

The sky on that first Christmas night was lit with a canopy of stars—and millions more beyond detection by the human eye. Yet one star guided the journey of the wise men from the Far East. Just one. These scholars knew the difference between this star and all the others that dotted the sky. This star was all they needed to find Him.

Whenever we place a beautiful shining star on the treetop, or suspend it high on the rooftop, it is a gleaming witness to the astronomical mystery that guided some of the wisest men alive in a journey of faith. It wasn't their intellect alone that persuaded them to travel in the dark. The Light—His Light—led them with every step, reminding them that

this birth wasn't just any birth. This baby King was the One the world had been waiting on!

The star is the one Christmas decoration that we know, beyond a doubt, was hung by the hands of the Creator of the universe for the arrival of His one and only Son. ❄

The lighted star (below left) that tops the Gaither family tree draws the eyes up to this shining symbol of the wise men's journey to their Savior. Throughout the Christmas season, the Gaithers' grape arbor (above) becomes a festival of lights shining on the path to their back door.

THE LIGHTS

In him was life,
and that life was the light of all mankind.

JOHN 1:4 NIV

Candles, twinkling lights, shining displays both indoors and out . . . lights of every kind cast their mesmerizing beauty throughout this season, transforming the appearance of our homes, our neighborhoods, our streets, and churches, our places of business for a few glorious weeks. We've all gathered the kids into

Anthony Burger was an enthusiastic communicator of The Song while he was with us, and he showed us that the music doesn't end when our time on earth does.

the car to take in the beautiful lights in our surrounding neighborhoods. Or sat in a darkened room just staring into the fire. Or gazed in wonder at the lights on the tree reaching out to us with their silent glow. Or been drawn in as Christmas Eve candles, one by one, multiply their light, suddenly dispelling the darkness. The welcoming lights of this season seem to emanate warmth, hospitality, joy, and peace. They draw not only our eyes but also our hearts, softening us somehow.

Of course, it isn't really the lights that soften us, but rather, all they represent: the Light of heaven, once untouchable and invisible, now suddenly flooding into our dark world and completely transforming it with perfect, eternal love. His life on earth was a beacon for our darkened understanding, and His stories shed light on concepts we couldn't have comprehended on our own. His presence still illuminates even the darkest reaches of our hearts, creating beauty there.

That is the miracle of Christmas—a miracle worth celebrating. When we light our candles and illuminate our homes and neighborhoods, we celebrate the Christ child, the man He became, and His Spirit, who still illuminates our every step. ❉

A Christmas candle is a lovely thing;
It makes no noise at all, but softly gives itself away.

EVA LOGUE

THE SONG

Worship so often erupts into song. It is the language of the angels, who spread the Good News to the hillsides that night. And Jesus' birth has kept the world singing ever since. There may be no more moving expression of worship than songs that help us celebrate the otherwise inexpressible things we hold so close during this Advent season.

Music—whether spiritual or just plain fun—makes the heart react whether it wants to or not. So sing your way through the holidays! Keep the music playing—whatever sets your heart and mind on the joy and irreplaceable memories of this most wonderful time of year. ❋

THE JOURNEY

Bearing gifts we travel afar . . .

REV. JOHN HENRY HOPKINS
"WE THREE KINGS"

Long before the days of GPS, three wise men packed their bags and headed west to follow the star that marked their destination. Their destination was Jesus!

Ours is too, really. And finding Jesus for us today means not only reveling in His love but lavishing that love on those around us, whether they live near or far. We journey to Grandmother's house or to see the kids because we know Christmas will not be the same without them.

So many happy memories are made when we set aside our everyday routine and go out of our way to share Christmas with loved ones, bringing gifts from afar (or even from just a few blocks away), finding a way to worship Him with the people He has given us as company on this journey through life. ❋

THE WARMTH

Later on, we'll conspire as we dream by the fire . . .

FELIX BERNARD
"WINTER WONDERLAND"

For much of the world, Christmas happens during the chilliest time of the year. And though it probably never snowed in Bethlehem on the night of Jesus' birth (or any other day of the year, for that matter), many of us are drawn to warm fires, steaming cider, and fresh soup to warm ourselves after braving the weather. These are the perfect conditions for huddling together with people we love and finding refuge. In some cultures, both past and present, a traditional Yule log made of long-burning hardwood is chosen and burned for hours of maximum warmth during the days or hours leading up to Christmas.

It is so tempting for the "doers" among us to get sidetracked with shopping lists and all the tasks we assign ourselves. But keeping warm together offers us the chance to just "be"—and to reflect on a Savior who came to earth to bring peace to His

Christmas just wouldn't be the same if we didn't go out of our way to bring greetings to the people we love (pictured left to right are Dean, Lexy, Karlye, and Kim Hopper). No one loves a good fire more than Bill (above), and he is thoroughly enjoying this fire with his granddaughter, Madeleine.

Worshiping
WITH ALL OUR SENSES
~ *Calvin Miller* ~

Is there any way we can ever get
the sacred and the secular to bend their knees
at a single altar? There is.
It is born in a single truth:
*Every good and every perfect gift
is from the Father above, coming down
from the Father of heavenly lights,
who does not change like shifting shadows.*
He chose to give us birth
through the word of truth (James 1:17).

Our worship is the great unifier of the chasm
between Santa Claus and the Holy Christ.
We have but to ask ourselves,
not, "Is this gift sacred or secular?"
but "Is this a good gift?"
And if it holds goodness, it is worthy
of our Christmas celebration.
Christ will not be embarrassed if we mention
snow and peppermint as we celebrate His
coming into human flesh.

Christmas is a time for loving God,
and all things in such a season will stir our
senses—all our senses:
smell, sound, sight, touch, and taste.
These five senses integrate our worship.
Forget sacred and secular, and
call the entire season one.

Continued on page 16

Solveig Leithaug's daughter, Kari Henderson, wasn't content to look out the window at this beautiful Christmas snow . . . she was drawn right into it.

people. Sharing a hot meal, a good cup of coffee, stories by the fireplace—these customs are perfect kindling for deepening our ties with one another and with the One who waits so eagerly for us to rest at His feet.

If we can picture our Savior as the inviting fire that beckons us to rest, fills us with His warmth, burns away all that is not important, and prepares us to go out into the cold world, Christmas becomes far less stressful and more deeply fulfilling than we could've imagined. ❄

THE SNOW

" Though your sins are like scarlet,
they shall be as white as snow."

ISAIAH 1:18 NIV

Not everyone gets to experience a white Christmas. But if you are so fortunate, you've surely had your breath taken away by the stark whiteness as it covers the earth in a sparkling blanket. Forgiving blemishes in the landscape and softening the ground and tree lines, snowflakes—as unique from each other as human beings

with our one-of-a-kind DNA—ban together to seemingly engulf the world in angel wings.

The gift of a fresh covering is a vivid image of the life we can experience through Immanuel. His coming, in a flurry of wonder and surprise, changed everything about the world as we know it. Though not always comfortable or predictable, a winter snow is a profound picture of the contrast found in our world before Christ—and after. He makes our weatherworn hearts as pure and beautiful as they were created to be. And aren't we grateful that He doesn't depart when the season is over! ❄

THE STORY

The laughter stops as
Pop picks up the Bible
It falls from habit to Luke 2
And none of us will ever
tire of hearing,
"Now children, here is how
God came to you."

"There were in that same
country shepherds watching
The flocks at night
upon lonely hill . . ."
And with his well-worn voice
he tells the story
Of how God loved us once
and loves us still.

WORDS BY GLORIA GAITHER
"CHRISTMAS IN THE
COUNTRY"

Music by William J. Gaither, Michael Sykes, Woody Wright. ©2000 Gaither Music Company, Mal 'N Al Music, Would He Write Songs. All rights controlled by Gaither Copyright Management. Used by permission.

Dressed in the Tennessee robe he got for Christmas, Levi Bowman sits in a circle with the Isaacs clan and takes his turn reading the Story from their family Bible.

Over and over again we hear it. Over and over again we tell it.

Never stop. This is the greatest story ever! The King of kings born in a smelly stable—to a virgin, His life endangered because of another jealous king, yet spared so He could ultimately sacrifice Himself to save us. Far better than any adventure, love story, or redemptive plot that could ever be born from the human imagination, this is God's Story—and it will be told for all eternity! It is a living story—still moving us the more we believe it, still changing us the more deeply we understand it.

Every time we hear it and every time we tell it, He is glorified. ❆

THE GIFTS

*Our gifts and those of the Magi
Do not hold the same prophetic weight,
But both are given in love
And both are good and perfect gifts
descended from the Father above.*

CALVIN MILLER

The gifts the wise men brought to Jesus carried both practical and prophetic significance. On the most practical level, these gifts served as a means of financial support for the young family. But their prophetic symbolism still reminds us of what Christ's coming meant to the world. Gold, a gift for royalty, represented His kingship. Frankincense, the aromatic oil burned in worship ceremonies, represented His priesthood. Myrrh, fragrant oil used to prepare bodies for burial, represented the sacrifice He would become for our sin.

The gifts we exchange with our loved ones might run more along the lines of aromatic candles, jewelry, or cologne, or perhaps bring thoughtful reminders of significant memories or hopes we share. Regardless of

how simple or elaborate, practical or luxurious, whether handmade or purchased, gifts are a tangible reminder that we are valued . . . known . . . loved.

The act of gift giving deserves thoughtful consideration. We are recipients of Christ's very best—His very life. Giving out of that blessing shines a sweet new light on the act of giving. Rather than a list to be checked off, our gifts are a beautiful, fragrant offering that represents far more than their tangible value! ❆

Lexi Hopper (right) gives her mommy, Kim, two beautiful things—a gift and a joyful smile.

THE FEAST

When Christ knew the time was drawing near to fulfill His mission as our Savior, He gathered his beloved disciples to break bread. After sharing the symbolism of the bread as His body, and the wine as His blood, Jesus urged these men that had traveled so many roads with Him, "Whenever you do this, do it in remembrance of me." He knew that for generations to

In anticipation of Christmas morning, the Phelps family sets out cookies by the fireplace for Santa and celery for his reindeer (below). Even now, the anticipation of Christmas is made extra-special at Janet's North Carolina home (bottom right) with this beautiful Christmas tree in her great room.

window and scratching frost off of it . . . I don't even know if there was frost since we were in Texas. But it seemed like it was cold, and I did my best to stay awake until I could see a red nose in the sky, because then I knew Rudolph was on his way!

I believed in all that. In the morning we'd wake up, having stayed up so late that we'd be rubbing our eyes. We have 8 mm home movies of us in our pajamas, rubbing our eyes as we walked down to see these things we thought Santa had brought, but that Mom and Dad had really just stayed up all night putting together. We couldn't come until they were ready. Then we would walk into the bright lights of the 8 mm camera . . . Do you remember that? Those were great memories! ✳

come, this combination of tastes—bread and drink—would always trigger memories of His sacrifice and the Love that motivated it.

This beautiful act of internalizing the Story is not entirely unlike the tradition of feasting as we celebrate His birth. Special tastes and combinations remind us of the hope-filled announcement of His miracle birth and the Love that came to rescue us. When we feast, it matters not what is on the table . . . but that we do this in remembrance of Him. ✳

ANTICIPATING
the Mystery

MARK LOWRY
Waiting for Christmas Morning

When I was a kid, I believed in Santa Claus. I mean, really believed in Santa Claus! And I would stay awake watching for him! I remember standing in my pajamas at the headboard of my bed, looking out the

 JANET PASCHAL
Transported by the
Touch of a Light Switch

When my sister and I were small, she usually awoke first on Christmas morning. But she would call me, and together we would tiptoe down the dark hall to the kitchen doorway. We would both find the light switch and flip it on. When the room lit up, it was almost more than we could bear: two kitchen chairs—one for each of us—holding items we had seen only in catalogs or on TV. They were

Worshiping
WITH ALL OUR SENSES
~ *Calvin Miller* ~

Consider the sound of sleigh bells
ringing out the joys of the season.
I wonder if their sound
Wasn't much like the sound of those bells
that dangled from a camel's bridle
in Matthew, chapter two.
A candied apple may be as sweet
as honey from the honeycomb,
fresh gathered from the jungles of
the Jordan River.

Make no division in the season.
Sense all of it at once!
Smell it, hear it, see it, touch it, taste it.
And suddenly everything is holy.
heaven's mercy inhabits the common things
as well as the grand.
Christmas! The adoration of all things
great and small.
A celebration of the senses.

there in front of us, close enough to touch, and the moment was electrifying.

For an entire year, we would anticipate Santa's largesse. We'd stand in long lines at Christmastime, eager to talk to him and offer our petitions. We'd mark items in books and point to toys in television commercials. We even left a piece of homemade cake for him, along with a note of gratitude.

When Kay and I touched the kitchen light switch, we were transported to a child's paradise. Meticulously examining the gifts stacked on the chairs, we could hardly contain our excitement … childhood versions of unbridled joy!

Our senses are now more keen, more refined. Yet nothing replicates the euphoria of those early Christmas mornings shared with my sister, courtesy of Santa. ❄

SOLVEIG LEITHAUG
Returning to the Tradition of Advent

Blending families also means blending traditions. Growing up Lutheran and being Norwegian, we—like most Norwegians—celebrated Advent. I had some years of attending churches where this was not celebrated, but as I began the journey of a new life with my husband, Jim, I was eager to again embrace this meaningful season that I learned is also important to him.

On the four Sundays leading up to Christmas, we will pause with the children for a few minutes at the dinner table, light a candle, maybe sing the verse of an Advent carol, and then read scriptures together.

This particular Advent candle ring (pictured at right) was Jim's and my first holiday purchase together. It is extra-special because we found it at a store in my hometown of Frekhaug, Norway (by Bergen) on the day he asked my dad (Peder Leithaug) for my hand in marriage. ❄

Solveig Leithaug and her family are now enjoying the tradition of Advent once again with the help of this beautiful Advent candle ring she and Jim purchased during a special visit to Norway.

The Sights
OF CHRISTMAS

❄ ❄ ❄

Ever since the shepherds were overwhelmed by a sky
full of singing angels and said to themselves, "Let's go
see this thing that has come to pass!" Christmas
has been a wonder we just have to witness with our own eyes!

The sight of a baby, born in a stable, resting on a nest of hay, made these same shepherds race out into the surrounding villages "glorifying and praising . . . God for all that they had heard and seen."

The wonder of Christmas is something we still want those around us to see. "Come over and see the tree," we say to our friends.

"Would you like to drive around with us to see the lights?" we invite our kids and grandkids.

"Hey, how about going with us to see the celebration in the city square?" we phone our neighbors.

"Have you seen the great display of gingerbread houses the county kids have built at the Minetrista Center?" we mention to someone at church.

"Would you like to go with our family to the live Nativity pageant at the country church near Noblesville?" we ask another mom after rehearsal for the Christmas program. "We could stop afterward and see the Christmas tree on the Circle and get some hot chocolate."

Lights, wreaths, pageants, angel choirs, stars, garlands, sparkling centerpieces; beautiful packages, colorful displays, street decorations, light shows . . . so much to see at Christmas that the whole world is eye candy.

What child hasn't stood in awe of the lights catching the crystals of freshly fallen snow and seen in them "fairies dancing on the night"? Or watched in wonder as skaters glide like angels over the ice at Rockefeller Center while magical snowflakes land on his tongue or get caught in her eyelashes?

Christmas is a carnival for the eyes. Come, look through the kaleidoscope of Christmas!

Gloria Gaither

Christmas...
EYES WIDE OPEN
~ Calvin Miller ~

Do you see what I see
Way up in the sky, little lamb?
Do you see what I see?
A star, a star, dancing in the night,
With a tail as big as a kite
With a tail as big as a kite?

NOEL REGNEY & GLORIA SHEYNE
"DO YOU HEAR WHAT I HEAR"

The eyes grow wide at Christmas.
The optic nerves work overtime.
They sort and categorize
the images of the season
and file them
under the category of "glorious."
There is so much to see, so many colors.
Red and green get bossy at this time of year,
but there are plenty of other colors too.
The entire palette of God is rich with color,
and He paints the very retina of our souls:
the gaudy regalia of the Magi—
blues, silvers, golds, and scarlets;
the rich earth-tones of the shepherds—
ochres and umbers, straws and thatch;
the jet-black skies alive with platinum angels
and the pinpricks of light-year stars
bleeding their titanium
through the canvas of the night.

Continued on page 25

THE BEAUTY *of* CHRISTMAS *at* HOME

BILL & GLORIA GAITHER
The Gaither Home at Christmas

The beauty of Christmas is best expressed at home. Not only in the way we decorate from the driveway and entry to every nook and cranny of the interior of our houses, but also in the atmosphere we create with music, lighting, food, fragrance, and attitude.

Bill and I collect Nativities from around the world, so the crèche is a focus in many of our rooms as well as in our outdoor decorations. For most families, the tree is central, and at Gaither Family Resources we display as many as

Over several years, Gaither employees gave us pieces to this life-sized Nativity.

twenty-five unique ideas for decorating "trees with a message" to suit almost any décor—from rustic to elegant, humorous to delightful.

Since we live in snow country, white trees frosted with icy glitter and hung with sparkling crystal orna-

The fireplace near the kitchen is a welcoming gathering place, brimming with evergreen and trimmed with red and lime green garland and lights (above). This white tree at Gaither Family Resources features doves, snow-encrusted branches, and other reminders of the peace the angels promised. (right).

ments are a favorite. One is accented with thin, white metal churches and words like *peace, joy,* and *love* to remind us of what Christ came to bring.

Another tree's snow-encrusted branches, white pine-cones, and life-sized doves suggest nature's silence and the promise of the Holy Spirit of peace that the angels proclaimed on that long-ago Judean hillside.

Close by is a regal tree in the purples of a king and the gold brought by the wise men, with the three kings from the Orient and their bedecked camels flanking the lower branches.

Stars and trumpet-shaped flowers in sky-blue and silver suggest that the very cosmos announces the coming to earth of a baby, the awesome Creator Himself!

A giant bronze Nativity accentuates another tree, elegantly covered with the deep, rich hues of dark cranberry, copper, and wine-colored ornaments.

Most important, though, is the telling and retelling of the Story, the greatest Story every told. Let's make sure our children understand each symbol: the star, the lights, the green of new life, the red of blood, the angels, the priceless gifts, the shepherds and sheep, the lowly stable and manger. Tell the Story with special food, and with every tree and centerpiece, every mantle and tradition. Share the meaning of every gift and song! ❄

The God of the universe
has "moved into the neighborhood"!
God is with us! Emmanuel!

LORI PHELPS
Decking the Halls at the Phelps Home

We make sure the Christmas boxes are pulled out of the barn before David's solo tour begins, which is usually the week before Thanksgiving. He does the heavy lifting, gets everything into the house, sets up the tree and the lights ... then I take over from there, except for the kids' tree in the kitchen. They do that ALL themselves—even the lights—and they hang up special ornaments they have made or collected over the years.

I put the ornaments on the other tree and decorate the mantles with magnolia clippings and evergreen from our property. I set the dining room table for Christmas, and it stays set throughout the season. From our light fixture I hang some beautiful handmade snowflakes—some of them a gift from the renowned designer Georg Anderson, who came and helped

us decorate for Christmas one year. His grandmother in Norway had crocheted the most incredible snowflakes, and he gave them to us! We treasure those.

We have several Nativity sets that are special because they were found during our travels, including one that David and I purchased in San Juan during our first Gaither cruise after he joined

the Vocal Band in February of 1998. That particular Nativity scene stays up year-round! We also treasure our set of three wise men made of olive wood that David's parents brought home for us from the Holy Land. But every Nativity set is special to us, even our kids' Fisher-Price sets! ❉

This is the kids' tree (left), which they set up, light, and decorate themselves with ornaments they have made or received over the years. The Phelps' table (above right) stays set throughout the season, and the handmade snowflakes hanging above it are treasured gifts.

CONNIE HOPPER
Christmas Cheer at the Old Family Farmhouse

Our old farmhouse that sheltered a family of nine during the 1940s could be transformed into a magical place at Christmas. It all began with cleaning. Mama's Christmas cleaning was equivalent to spring cleaning: everything had to be just right—in its place and spic-and-span in preparation for the decorating.

Once the house was how she wanted it, we went to a place on our farm where evergreen vines grew along the ground, and there we gathered enough of what she called "running cedar" to hang above every window and doorsill in the house. We also went to the back pasture for trimmings from the holly trees with beautiful red berries. We'd cut enough small branches to add to the cedar. The smell of cedar permeated the whole house, and the freshness of the green garland, holly leaves, and berries were beautiful to see.

The Christmas tree was a cedar from the farm. This only added to the wonderful vision of Christmas. Decorations for the tree were the same ornaments year after year. Simple, but how special they were! As we lit the tree and our daddy led us in "Silent Night" and "Joy to the World," that old farmhouse was filled with love. And, yes, to this child, it was filled with the magic of Christmas. ❅

All the decorations around the Gardner home (this page) hold history—special places they have traveled, loved ones who gave them as gifts, or things their girls or grandson have made.

Joy Gardner
Heirlooms: Decorating with Memories

To begin our holiday festivities, I always place candles in all the windows. I take out the Christmas china (which we actually *do* use every day throughout the season); I turn on my favorite Christmas music; and I set out a new puzzle for nieces, nephews, and guests who will be coming by during the holidays.

Our Christmas decorations reflect the personalities of everyone in our family. Each of us has our favorite things that we want to set out to remind us of our special memories.

Our tree, mantle, staircase, and table—with their greenery, ribbons, pinecones, flowers, twinkle-lights, and candles—all create a timeless feel. The same stockings that have hung on the fireplace since our girls were small still hang there, waiting for Christmas morning surprises. For the past thirty years, we have collected ornaments from all over the world—from Vienna to Alaska, New York to Pigeon Forge—and our tree is a patchwork of those travel memories combined with the crafts that our children, and now our grandson, have made throughout the years.

Our table is set with cherished gifts that have been given to us, like Baccarat and Waterford crystal angels. One year, as we were pulling out our decorations, Landy commented that it was nice that we had two beautiful sets of angels—one for each of our daughters. I asked him which was his favorite, and he said, "The Baccarat, I think." We had no idea anyone was listening, but from upstairs we faintly heard Lauren say, "The Baccarat is mine!" ❅

JEFF & SHERI EASTER
Oh, Yes, We Need a Little Christmas!

My routine of decorating for the holidays begins Thanksgiving Day, with Jeff pulling the outdoor wreaths, garland, and red bows out of storage. He helps with all of the decorations that require a ladder and then leaves the rest to me.

We begin with the outdoors. I hand-tie the bows and straighten each twig on the garland swags that drape the porch handrails and front door. We also hang a special wreath on the door, and simple pine wreaths on the bay windows and dormers. We decorate the gazebo with pine garland and red bows, and put a lighted white Christmas tree in the center. Two lighted reindeer sit in front of the gazebo, and some whimsical Santa and candy-cane decorations line the side entrance of the house especially for the kids. At the back door, the family entrance is decorated with garland, wreaths, and bows and is a lot less formal and

> IT TAKES ME SEVERAL DAYS TO DECORATE, BUT IT'S ALL DONE WITH CHRISTMAS MUSIC PLAYING.

more "Santa-fied" for Maura, our youngest, to enjoy!

Inside, my front foyer has garland swag up the staircase with turquoise, fuchsia, lime, and red balls, trimmings, and leopard-print ribbon and peacock feathers. We have a tree to match, covered only with hand-blown glass ornaments that we have selected as a family over the past twenty-six years. The Nativity set that we purchased for our first Christmas sits on a table just as you enter.

Our dining room is filled with special Christmas items given to us through the years by close friends and family. One of my favorites is a tree full of beautiful ornaments that tell the Christmas story, which were given to us by Bill and Gloria Gaither about fifteen years ago.

In our kitchen, the table is laden with Christmas china and matching cloth napkins and candles. I have a small tree with beaded fruit and a garland swag over the entrance to the den that matches our main tree, which is located next to the fireplace in the den. The colors are the same, but this is the tree that houses all of our hand-made ornaments and collectibles that represent us as a family—first Christmas together; baby's first Christmas;

It doesn't snow often in Georgia, so this rare photo captures the Easters' snow-covered home all decked out for Christmas.

first Christmas in our home; St. Thomas, Alaska, London, Paris, Australia, South Africa, Ireland, Jerusalem, Norway, Germany, and many other wonderful places we've visited over the years. Carolers surround our piano, and Maura has her favorite stuffed musical Santa, reindeer, and snowmen sitting around the tree.

This Christmas tree in the foyer contains hand-blown glass ornaments the Easter family has collected for more than a quarter-century.

Our stockings are all handmade. For my first Christmas, a friend of our family's made me a stocking of red and white felt with cute cutouts and beads. My mama used that stocking for me every year and then gave it to me when I got married. I chose to keep using it, and created one to match mine for Jeff, but with slight differences. As my children were born, I made each of them their own matching stockings—and all five hang from our fireplace mantle. My first Santa and Rudolph are also a part of the tradition, now in their forty-seventh year.

My girls have always had special trees they decorate in their bedrooms. Morgan's is cute and teenager-themed, while Maura's is a Barbie tree!

I have been known to put up as many as eight trees in a year, but the older I get, the more quality time I put into my favorite trees. It takes me several days to decorate, but it's all done with Christmas music playing in the background while I "disappear" into the holidays each year, creating Christmas for the ones I love. ✳

KIM HOPPER
Elegance with Flair

My usual Christmas decorating starts as close to Thanksgiving as possible. I want to make Thanksgiving its own

---

Christmas…
EYES WIDE OPEN
~ Calvin Miller ~

The first Christmas left the shepherds
wide-eyed and overwhelmed
by a sky full of winged messengers
that bathed their dull, working night
in visions so glorious they
began crying to each other,
"Let's go see this thing that has come to pass,
which the Lord has made known to us."

❧

Then came the wonder
for which God made
all optic nerves and retinas.
Their eyes blinked
like the shutters of a modern camera
when they saw Him,
Jesus, the infant Son of God,
snuggled into a nest of hay.
And they were hushed by the sight.

❧

But when the hush subsided,
They ran out into
the surrounding villages,
glorifying God for all they had seen.
How like those shepherds we are.
Bewildered by the wonder
of simply seeing.

Continued on page 32

Anthony Burger's cherished Christmas in the City villages stretch into many rooms of the house and are largely comprised of treasured gifts from his fans over the years. This "Anthony Burger Signature Grand Piano" ornament (bottom) was created in Anthony's memory by Ornaments to Remember.

special holiday, but I don't mind having the trees trimmed while sitting down for a wonderful meal with our family.

I typically pull everything from the attic and put up small trees in our daughters' rooms, set the festive floral arrangements in their designated places, and find just the right spot for the multiple Santas and special holiday figurines. Next, I bring in my good friend and professional decorator, Brandon Beene. He's very well known among the Homecoming friends and has assisted a lot of artists with finishing touches on their holiday decor. Brandon and I put up two big, special trees and wrap the banister with garland and bows, welcoming Santa to the holiday.

I use mostly traditional colors of green, red, and gold in my décor; however, we make everything unique with rich fabrics, greenery, extravagant bows, heavy mosaic ornaments, and even fun feathers here and there! I love classy, traditional, elegant decorations with a flair!

Christmas music can typically be found playing, and the kids running in and out of the house, as my husband, Dean, and the girls decorate the outside. There are wreaths and faux candles in the windows; the front porch is wrapped with garland and bows; and a few lighted Christmas trees are placed strategically on the lawn. It feels like Christmas just writing about it! Think I'll go to the attic and bring down a few things. ❄

Luann Burger
Christmas Collections

Each year we look forward to getting started with the decorating tradition, which doesn't begin until Christmas music is playing throughout the house on the intercom system. Imagine more than thirty large plastic storage bins, nine Christmas trees, and a designated overhead garage loft filled with all the decorations. That is what we uncrate each year in early November. Most years, the house display is completed two weeks before Thanksgiving, giving us many weeks to enjoy

the beauty of the holiday season. It is not unusual for our home to still be decorated until mid-January.

One of our favorite collections is Anthony's prized Christmas in the City villages. Each room in our home has a themed collection, including several New York City locations, old-town buildings, and landscapes. Many of these villages were gifted by Anthony's fans and have extreme sentimental value.

Our stairway is adorned with garlands embellished with gold and burgundy accents that complement the living-room Christmas tree—a frequently favored setting for photos. This tree is adorned with many nostalgic items dating back to "First Christmas Together" ornaments, the kids' first Christmas decorations, and the "Anthony Burger Signature Grand Piano" ornament created in his memory by Ornaments to Remember.

This past season, my daughter Lori persuaded me to go with a more modern tree design, and I have to admit: the black, silver, and red decorations were absolutely stunning. ❆

Family Fest. Quite a conversation piece . . . and it was great because it left plenty of room underneath for all those presents! Outside, Jimmy framed the entire house with thousands of lights. It glowed so brightly and beautifully. And it looked 3-D!

Of course putting everything up is the fun part. Taking it all down always makes us a little sad. I guess that's why it takes us almost till spring to do it! ❆

How do you decorate an upside-down Christmas tree (above)? Like this! Sonya and Jimmy's house, with its amply lit exterior (bottom left), reflects their deep-down love for this beautiful season. The Hampton boys (below) get in on the decorating too, with trees just their size.

SONYA ISAACS-YEARY
Going All Out

I love to decorate the house for the holidays! Snowman doo-dads, Santa Claus knick-knacks, stockings, Christmas china, pine- or sugar cookie-scented candles, and so much more! I have about a dozen pieces of the Snow Village collection, which I absolutely love to set out. Last year, for the first time, we set up an upside-down Christmas tree that we got in Gatlinburg during

WES HAMPTON
Decorating Duties at the Hampton House

Andrea's in charge of the decorations. She always decorates the majority of the Christmas tree, except for the lower portion, which the boys decorate with ornaments. She also sets out lots of little snowmen (she loves snowmen) throughout the house, along with many other decorations.

I'm not allowed to mess with the indoor decorations;

The Hampton family Christmas tree. The Bowman's peppermint-themed tree (right).

I'm in charge of hanging the lights outside the doorway and down our entryway. I also put out a lighted train in the front yard that the boys always love. I don't go all "Clark Griswold" on anybody, but I do enjoy having plenty of lights. I'm not brave enough to line the roof with those icicle lights, but I am thinking of hiring someone to do that! ✳

ANDY ANDREWS
Thanksgiving until New Year's

Because we love Christmas so much, our family squeezes every bit of time out of our decorated house that we possibly can. Decorating begins the day after Thanksgiving. No ifs, ands, or buts—once the turkey's gone, the Christmas holiday begins. We always put up our tree on that Friday, and it does not come down until New Year's (which means a lot of regular and frequent watering!).

This past year, we decided to put lights up in the front yard. Because that's such a big job, we cheated and started assembling it all before Thanksgiving. But we didn't turn the lights on until the day after Thanksgiving. ✳

REBECCA ISAACS BOWMAN
Honoring the Heritage

At Christmastime, my home has a few different themes. My Christmas tree displays the peppermint theme: red and white. I love the boldness of the red against the solid white. Plus, peppermint smells divine and looks even better.

I also love to decorate my home with different styles of menorahs. The Hanukkah story is so uplifting and full of miracles; I want to keep the Jewish heritage alive and pass down the beautiful Hanukkah tradition. ✳

BUDDY GREENE
Decorating at the Greenes'

We usually start pulling out the Christmas decorations shortly after Thanksgiving Day. By "we," I mean Vicki and the girls. I usually just get called on for any heavy lifting—pulling boxes off the storage shelves, bringing home the Christmas tree and setting it up, or keeping the fire going. You know, the grunt work. But we all love to see the house transformed with the colors, symbols, and smells of Christmas. By the first week or so of December there are angels, Santas, creches, red and green everywhere, and practically nothing but Christmas music is played on the stereo. ✳

JASON CRABB
The Crabb Tree

It's a lot of fun around our house! The kids and I put up two trees: one in the front foyer, and one in the living room. The girls love to put on the ornaments. Of course, they also love to hang them all on one limb! That's usually how it works! But they do a wonderful job of taking the little ornaments and putting them on. They love doing that. I, on the other hand, never look forward to bringing all that stuff out, but once it's up, it's always a joyous time.

My wife, Ashley, then takes tons of shiny beads and wraps them up and down the banister. And we've got some of those inflatables that we put out on the front porch. The outside's also got a light-up wreath and other lights . . . the kids love that stuff! ✳

"Perhaps the best Yuletide decoration
is being wreathed in smiles."

AUTHOR UNKNOWN

Shine *Your* Lights

"I am the light of the world.
If you follow me, you won't have to walk in darkness."

JOHN 8:12 NLT

MARK LOWRY
Lighting the Palm Trees

"If it can't be hired done, it doesn't get done!" That's what I say!

I suppose the main way I decorate is with lights. I put up white lights all around the house. I even wrap lights around the palm trees that I have by the pool, making them glow all white. I like white! ❄

LADYE LOVE SMITH
Lights and Memories

I remember so vividly decorating for Christmas. Every year, my daddy would put this big red sleigh with a waving Santa and reindeer out on our front lawn. I loved this and looked forward to it every year. I knew he would be tired coming home from work, but I could always count on him to make the decorating a big deal and a great memory for me. We would put the lights up too; and my mom would be inside, baking and cooking incredible treats with *A Charlie Brown Christmas* or *Rudolph the Red-nosed Reindeer* on TV, or with beautiful Christmas music playing.

My mother always took my sister and me to Memphis to Goldsmith's to see the Enchanted Forest and to buy us Christmas dresses (and shoes!) for church. And my daddy would take me "downtown" to Iuka to see Santa at Sears!

Going to my grandparents' house on Christmas Eve is a big memory for me. I would be so excited, and on the way I would try to count how many colored lights I could see. I remember laughing, playing with my cousins, and eating wonderful food while we were there. Then we would pray together and read the story of Christmas from the Bible. On the way home I would lie in the back of my parents car and try so hard to go to sleep quickly, hoping that Santa would come before we got home! Secretly, I would be looking up in the sky, watching for a sleigh and eight tiny reindeer! ❄

The light display at Mark Lowry's Spanish-style Texas home (left) is a warm, welcoming sight at Christmas. Ladye and her dad still share many Christmas memories. He is pictured here (below) with grandson, Bret, in front of Reggie and Ladye's Nashville home.

The Captivating Christmas Tree

REBA RAMBO McGUIRE
The Peppermint Tree

We were so poor that poor people called us poor. We lived in a little shotgun Kentucky house, but it was cozy with crisp curtains and hand-sewn slipcovers Mom created with great tenderness and skill. There were always fragrant flowers artfully arranged, big bowls of brightly colored fresh fruit, and yummy homemade treats tempting me on Grandmother's tiered crystal compote.

Even though we were poor, I didn't know it.

You could ask anybody... our house was the cleanest one on the block. Mom could wear out the Lysol, Pine-Sol, baking soda, bleach, and apple cider vinegar; germs didn't stand a chance! She taught me at a very young age the joy of a clean, welcoming, and peaceful environment.

Without a doubt, Christmas was the most highly anticipated and celebrated childhood holiday. Talk about stimulating the senses! The mingled aromas of pine, spruce, gingerbread, caramel corn, and stuffed turkey; oh, the wondrous sounds of carolers, church bells ringing, and "Merry Christmas" greetings from young and old alike. It was the very best time of the year!

Mom and Dad usually came off the road about the

Christmas...
EYES WIDE OPEN
~ *Calvin Miller* ~

"Come and see Christmas."
The invitations come from everywhere,
from friends and family,
coworkers and neighbors.

❧

Seeing Christmas is a special wonder.
God ennobles the common eye to
drink its fill of splendor:
there is so much to behold, so much to see,
a cornucopia of images
from candles' glow and red carnations
to gift-wrapped packages,
laser shows, snowflakes
and skaters ice-gliding across a pond.

❧

The God of Christmas is
the God of optic nerves.
And this Vesuvius of wonders began in
centuries long gone,
when a baby cried and
a young mother sang the first of the
Yuletide anthems:
My soul doth magnify the Lord,
and my spirit rejoices in God my Savior,
for the Lord has done great things for me,
and Holy is His name.

second week in December, and after a day or two of rest, the festivities began. Dad and I would search diligently for the perfect tree: seven feet tall; very full; a dark, rich color with damp needles . . . and it had to call out my name! (Don't even ask.)

Mom's creative talent flourished as she crafted unusual decorations from lace, metallic foil paper, scraps of velvet, and a potpourri of lovely feathers and materials. While she was the designer for many of our ornaments, Dad and I were the ones who decided how and where they were strategically placed on the tree.

We spent many happy hours decorating and being serenaded by Christmas carols from our stereo: the Ray Coniff Singers, George Beverly Shea singing Christmas hymns, 101 Strings, Bing Crosby, Rosemary Clooney,

> I KNEW IT WAS
> A STRETCH EACH YEAR
> FOR ENOUGH MONEY
> TO HAVE EVEN ONE TREE.

and Handel's *Messiah*. I use the term "stereo" very loosely, since it was a $39.95 phonograph turntable with built-in speakers. After the tree trimming, Dad would usually take a favorite book off the shelf and settle in his comfy chair for the evening. (My dad may be a country gospel crooner, but he has always been a lover of classical music, timeless literature, and fine art. I guess I was learning a lot about culture in those hills and didn't even realize it at the time.)

The Friday night before Christmas, we usually hosted a party for a few friends and family—a party that was, in reality, a holiday jam session. Those hard-working coal miners, farmers, and grocery store clerks transformed into uninhibited, talented musicians. Just put a guitar or fiddle in their hands and stand back! They sang and played from their souls for the sheer joy of the music. We belted out all the Christmas songs with gusto and conviction till long after midnight . . .

One such night, I felt an overwhelming desire for my own Christmas tree, but I kept that desire to myself. I knew it was a stretch each year for enough money to have even one tree. But still, I couldn't stop dreaming: wouldn't it be grand to snuggle down in the plump feather bed and stare at my own little tree twinkling atop the antique dresser?

I don't know if I talked in my sleep or if Dad invaded my dreams, but that Christmas Eve morning, I couldn't believe it! My very own tree was glistening there, emanating the sugar-sweet aroma of Mr. Dixon's Candy Store. I threw back the patchwork quilt, leapt out of bed, and started jumping up and down, clapping my hands with glee. Though it was the most unusual tree, it was prettier to me than the White House Christmas tree!

When Mom and Dad heard all the commotion, they came running to my room. Mom explained: "Your dad journeyed into the woods and found these beautifully proportioned branches, dragged them home, stripped off the dead leaves, and spray-painted each one with white enamel. He planted them in my big red enamel flowerpot, wrapped every branch candy-cane style with thin ribbon, and added a string of flickering, miniature lights. Don't you just love the peppermint candy canes and the satin-red ornaments?"

"I thought the two little robins perched on the branches were the perfect finishing touch," Dad grinned. "I've watched the way you sit for hours staring at our Christmas tree and writing your poetry. I just thought it might be nice to have this little peppermint tree in your room to inspire even more creativity."

I threw my arms around him and gave him a tight hug. I had never felt more loved in my life. I had to be the richest girl in Kentucky! ❊

MICHAEL ENGLISH
The English Family Tree

One of our traditions is to always decorate the tree as a family. It came from Marcie's childhood, and it was something so important to her that she insisted we have that special time too. So every year she gets everything out, and she and Bella and I decorate the tree together while eating Christmas cookies and listening to Christmas music. It is a very special time for our family. ❊

Bella English proudly shows off the beautiful tree she helped decorate and the ornament with a picture of her and her daddy.

Tanya and her sister April in their front yard in Madisonville, Kentucky.

store-bought treasures given to us by kids we taught in Sunday school.

Michael and I have a tradition of buying an ornament for each year we've been together. Not necessarily a dated "collector" ornament, but something that represents that year to us. There's one we bought on our first Alaskan cruise; there's a little house-shaped one in 1986, the year we purchased our first home; a tiny pink ceramic baby shoe for Mallory's first Christmas; and a stack of baby blocks for Aly's. ✳

TANYA GOODMAN-SYKES
Christmas Trees through the Years

Growing up, we didn't get a lot of white Christmases, so it was quite a treat when we did. If you look closely at the photo above, you can see our AWESOME silver aluminum Christmas tree through the window. I LOVED that thing! We had the whole works, complete with the lighted turning color wheel. Oh, we were so hip!

Our family tree now doesn't have a theme or fancy ribbons or magnolia blossoms or anything . . . and some of my decorations are almost as old as I am! I have some beautiful handmade felt ornaments that some Happy Goodman Family fans made for my dad when I was just a girl. There are painted Popsicle-stick stars and golden pinecone decorations my kids made in school. We also have a hodge-podge of handmade and

CHARLOTTE RITCHIE
An Ornament a Year

Christmas is my favorite time of year, so when it comes to decorating, our family jumps in with both feet. We have a nine-foot Christmas tree with hundreds of clear lights. I love angels, so many of the ornaments are angel-themed. Every year we buy a new family ornament and the kids each get a new ornament. Landon's are train-themed, and so far, Jayna has been all about the princess ornaments!

We decorate as a family—we drink apple cider and listen to Christmas music as we work. It's a great tradition that I hope will be a wonderful memory for our children. ✳

Each year, as Landon and Jayna (above) grow, so does the collection of ornaments on Greg and Charlotte Ritchie's family Christmas tree.

City Sights

SONYA ISAACS-YEARY
City Sidewalks

There's nothing more amazing to me than Christmas in New York City! Ever since I was a little girl, we have taken trips there to visit my grandmother in the Bronx, usually in December. Oh, the atmosphere in the Big Apple at Christmastime! Rockefeller Center proudly displaying its giant Christmas tree . . . ice skaters bundled up in their scarves and gloves, going 'round and 'round to the sounds of classic Christmas songs . . . the bigger-than-life ornaments decorating the streets and hanging from the stoplights . . . and of course my favorite: the festive holiday displays filling the windows of the department stores like Barney's, Saks Fifth Avenue, Bloomingdale's, and so many others. New York City truly captures the spirit of Christmas in every sense of the word! ❄

Sonya and Jimmy enjoy the sights of New York City at Christmas. Pictured here is their stop at Rockefeller Center.

LILY ISAACS
Manhattan Memories

The earliest memory I have of Christmas is when my family and I would go to Manhattan to shop, and we would see the many beautiful decorations in the Saks' and Macy's store windows. We'd also go ice skating at Rockefeller Center.

The sights and sounds of Christmas were very exciting. There were the vendors with umbrellas on top of their stands that said "Sabret," selling hot dogs with sauerkraut (though the most distinct smell to me was the hot chestnuts cooking at these little stands).

I always knew it was Christmas when I went to Manhattan. We even had the privilege to see the Rockettes at Radio City Music Hall a couple of times. That was truly a Christmas extravaganza! ❄

JOE BONSALL
Comforted by the Light

I grew up in a rowhouse on Jasper Street in Philadelphia, Pennsylvania. My bedroom window faced an alleyway—a perfect view of about forty small backyards. But I could also see the fronts of some of the houses on a street about a block away. There was a house on Emerald Street with decorations that really lit up their modest porch. Blinking lights of all colors and one bright, white, shining star on their rooftop completed the picture.

During the Christmas season I could lay propped up on a pillow on my bed, lift the window shade, and watch the lights and the shining star from that house a block away. As a little boy growing up among the streets, it seemed I was always looking for some magic and emotion, and I took great comfort in that little lighted star. It seemed to light up the back alley with promise and goodness, warmth and hope. I guess I was a crazy kid, but somehow it worked for me.

I have grown up to be a crazy adult as well, and I still find myself seeking Light. God's blessings are all around us at Christmas . . . and always! We only need to be open-minded and open-hearted. ❋

The Wonder *of* Nature

WES HAMPTON
Dreaming of a White Christmas

I grew up in West Tennessee, where it was hot and humid a good portion of the year. Obviously, snow wasn't something we experienced very often. And the chance of us actually getting snow at Christmas was slim-to-none. Though around 7:00 one Christmas Eve, right after our church's candlelight service ended, it began snowing. It snowed the entire night. The next morning when we awoke to open our presents, I remember looking outside to see our entire three-acre yard completely covered in a blanket of clean, bright snow. Christmas 2010 was also a special one because we had a white Christmas . . . in Birmingham, Alabama! It was the first white Christmas on record. Our boys had a blast! ❋

Barrett and Hudson Hampton enjoy this rare white Christmas in Birmingham.

GLORIA GAITHER
The Cardinal

The cardinal (*cardinalis cardinalis*) is the Indiana state bird. Its habitat is woodland edges, thickets, and, thankfully, suburban gardens and wooded village lawns. Its song is distinctive and welcome in the dark mornings of winter. *The Peterson Field Guide* describes this song as "clear, slurred whistles, lowering in pitch," but any gospel-music lover would call it a "signature lick." It could be described as *what-cheer-cheer* or *whoit-whoit-whoit*, sounding a lot like a question inviting our response.

The male bird is the most startling crimson red, while the female is a warm brown with a red edge on her painted crest and a red border on her graceful wings. In both, the dark face and heavy triangular red bill are distinctive.

When Indiana days are cold and dim; when the once-lush maples, sweet gums, oaks, and sycamores are bare skeletons against a gray sky; when the pines are black and the snow has covered all green with a thick blanket of white, the glorious cardinal swoops across the dull landscape with a red so brilliant it never ceases to surprise the eye. The silence is broken by the song of "What-cheer-cheer!" and the interrogative "Whoit? Whoit?" coaxes an answer from the most discouraged of hearts.

Right now, at Christmas, the answer must be "Hope!" The crimson answer to the darkest of worlds is always hope! Red to punctuate the gray of winter. Red to remind us all that the Crimson Tide of heaven has come into our world to surprise the dullest of hearts with the message: Be of good cheer; I have overcome the world! ❄

JEFF HAWES
of Karen Peck & New River
Christmas in the Dark

Christmas is without a doubt my favorite holiday. There's just something about seeing everyone dressed in red and green, the smell of hot apple cider and cinnamon, the taste of gingerbread cookies and milk, and the feelings of warmth and love as we sing carols around a cozy fire. The idea of celebrating Jesus in the dark doesn't usually come to mind. But one year we learned that when the lights are out and the music stops and the oven comes to a halt, the focus shifts to the true meaning of it all.

My mom is the baby of eight children, and there is never a dull moment at her family's Christmas Eve gathering. I can still remember how much I anticipated the party we would have at my uncle's house when I was a child. Uncle Bill would play his guitar, Aunt Carolyn would play the piano, and all the siblings would line up across the living room as "Blue Christmas"—the signature song of the night—would be sung.

Usually, the highlight of the night was when MawMaw Jeffery would open her gifts. It was always a spectacle! Some years she would get a mixture of beautiful clothes and jewelry, but sometimes my uncle would slip a fake snake or lizard in her box, and the place would come alive! Oh, how I wish I could go back in

MAWMAW PASSED AWAY SHORTLY AFTER THIS CHRISTMAS PARTY, BUT THOSE FEW MOMENTS IN THE DARK WILL FOREVER GLOW IN MY HEART.

time! Little did I know, 2010 would be my last year to watch MawMaw open gifts.

Last year, Christmas Eve was a different celebration. With chances of a thunderstorm on the loose, many in the family decided to spend Christmas at home, not wanting to risk their lives in the storm. MawMaw wouldn't miss it for the world. For the past few years she had been living in a nursing home because she was unable to take care of herself, her mind quickly fading. So for her, a chance to get out of Hall D was a dream come true.

As the few of us crazy enough to brave the elements started piling in at my uncle's house, I noticed MawMaw sitting in her usual chair, except this time she wasn't laughing or joking around. It was as if she was soaking it all up. Did she know it would be her last Christmas Eve party with us?

Later that night, we ate delicious food. What a spread we had! I noticed Mom feeding MawMaw her favorite chicken and dressing and creamed potatoes. As we were eating, the lights began to flicker. Once. Twice. Gone. I couldn't believe that of all nights, the power had to go out on Christmas Eve. We finished our meal by candlelight, and I imagine we weren't the first ones to experience this.

Although all the rest of us were unhappy that the lights were out and the music had stopped and the oven couldn't be used, MawMaw never changed her expression. She didn't mind; she was just where she wanted to be.

And she was right—the evening wasn't ruined after

all. We sang "Silent Night" and "Away in a Manger" and a few other carols that night, but I don't think they could've sounded any better if we'd had a hundred people in that room. Shutting our eyes and just imagining what it must have been like to celebrate Jesus' birth so many years before, made it more special this year.

As we finished singing, I knew it was time to open MawMaw's gifts, and so did she. You could see her eyes light up in the sparkle of the candles as she gazed at the packages around her. However, this year she couldn't reach down to pick them up or even remove the wrapping paper. As I watched her try to accomplish what she had always been so great at doing, it brought me to tears. I went over and sat beside her chair and began opening the gifts for her.

You can imagine it was tough opening presents by candlelight, and it was especially hard reading those cards. As I opened gift after gift for MawMaw, I couldn't see her response too well, but I could feel her loving hands as she touched each item, each piece of jewelry—almost as if she was feeling each intricate design. When we finished unwrapping the gifts, I kissed her on the cheek and told her I loved her. I'm not certain she knew my name that night, but the familiarity of her hug and the smell of her Elizabeth Taylor perfume seemed to be just enough.

I was reminded that night that Christmas is about Jesus. He wants us to take enough time out of our busy schedules to worship Him, love our family, and make memories. My childhood memories are what I live on—they are my food, my survival.

MawMaw passed away shortly after this Christmas party, but those few moments in the dark will forever glow in my heart. ❄

MICHAEL ENGLISH
Transformation: Seeing Christmas through the Eyes of Love

After I lost everything in my life, Christmas became a painful part of my year. I would spend Christmas Eve walking around the mall, looking at all the decorations and festivities and watching other families smiling and laughing. It hurt. But I would go there because it was the only way I could see a little bit of what I used to feel as a child, or when I had a family of my own.

When I married Marcie, I was delighted to find out that she and her family make Christmas a very big deal. They are all about the traditions, the togetherness. It's the best time of year for me now.

Specifically, though, one year after Marcie and I had just built and moved into our new home, and our daughter, Bella, was about three years old, I went on the road for a solo weekend. When I came home and walked in the door, the first thing I smelled was a most delicious pot roast that Marcie had been cooking all day. Then I began to hear the sound of Christmas music playing in the background. I'll never forget— it was Harry Connick Jr. singing.

> NO LONGER DID I HAVE TO PICTURE THOSE LONELY NIGHTS AT THE MALL. I HAD A NEW PICTURE...

Then, as I walked farther in, my eyes were instantly drawn to the beautiful Christmas decorations and tree that Marcie had put up while I was gone. She ran over to me and hugged and kissed me, and then my ears heard the sound of sweet little feet running down the stairs and a voice yelling, "Daddy, Daddy!"

It was a moment that froze me in time. I instantly flashed back to those lonesome days of walking around the mall by myself. Then I looked at the vision in front of me—my beautiful wife, my precious daughter held close, the beauty of my home. I was overwhelmed with the feeling of being the most blessed man on the planet. No longer did I have to picture those lonely nights at the mall. I had a new picture—one that embodies the closeness and the true meaning of this very special time of year!

The Sounds
OF CHRISTMAS

❋ ❋ ❋

Music defines Christmas—
not just the music of Christmas carols filling the house
and the age-old story set to a hundred different tunes,
but the music and rhythms of life.

The giggles and whispers of children keeping secrets.

Resounding bells coming from the Salvation Army bell ringers in front of the grocery store.

The crinkling of paper being folded around surprise packages.

Melodious carolers singing in the crisp winter night.

The music of traffic in the streets, the passengers rushing home with gifts.

Logs crackling in the fireplace and the hot bubbling of chili simmering on the stove.

Who can keep from humming along to this harmonious song of life? Christmas is one time when everything winds down for a magical moment to retell the greatest story ever told. The Giver of the music first started the whole world singing this song with an angel chorus, and the Song will never be satisfied until all creation joins in at the greatest Homecoming this world—and the entire cosmos—has ever known.

SINGING ALTO

BY AMY GAITHER-HAYES

Sitting next to my mother
singing number three hundred fifty nine
- I Am the Lord's I Know -
a smooth third beneath the melody line
her deep voice a sonorous vibration
against my ear
- Whether I live or die -
- Whether I wake or sleep -
learning the alto line was not so
much a choice as this is how you sing
a hymn if you are a woman
in a church full of men, full of
ladies singing high, clear, right on the
obvious melody, full of basses
and baritones and tenors
but if you are different
if you understand that your part is to
give the melody something to lean on
if you understand that not everyone gets the spotlight
but without you, the song is thin and frail
if you understand that your value is in your belonging,
your place in this family, your being loved, your belovedness
not in singing high, singing loud, singing in the main part
if you understand this
then maybe, maybe you too, can learn
the alto, a third below, smooth and sonorous enough
for a child to sleep comfortably, lulled to sleep by the
vibration
the sound of belovedness

EXCERPTED FROM *A COLLECTION OF WEDNESDAYS*, WRITTEN BY AMY GAITHER-HAYES.

Hearing CHRISTMAS
~ *Calvin Miller* ~

Long ago, in another context, I wrote,
"No shot was ever heard around the world.
In fact, in all of human history
only two sounds have been
heard around the world. The first was
a baby's cry, saying, 'It has begun.'
And the second was the cry of a carpenter,
crying, 'It is finished!'
And between these two cries was the
Greatest Story Ever Told!"
It is a story that, as the Gaithers have long
reminded us,
started the whole world singing
His Song.

❧

There could be no real Christmas without music.
Who has not been hushed by the majesty of
the "Hallelujah Chorus"?
And who has not been touched by the
composer's testimony?
"Come walk with me through fields
and forests;
We'll climb those hills, and still hear that song,
For even hills resound with music,
They just can't help it, God gave the song." *

Continued on page 55

* Excerpted from "God Gave the Song."
Words by Gloria Gaither and Ronn Huff.
Music by William J. Gaither and Ronn Huff.
© 1969 by Gaither Music Company and Paragon Music Corp.

THE VOICES OF CAROLERS

The earth has grown old with its burden of care
But at Christmas it always is young,
The heart of the jewel burns lustrous and fair
And its soul full of music breaks the air,
When the song of angels is sung.

PHILLIPS BROOKS

DAVID & LORI PHELPS
Caroling as a Family

Every year, without fail, our family goes caroling together. It has become the one thing that we just can't miss, and the kids look forward to it as much as the adults! A few years ago, when we knew this would become an annual tradition, we finally created our own family Christmas songbooks and the kids decorated the front covers.

With David's tour schedule and our family's busy schedules, it varies from year to year when we can go or how many of us are able to make it. Whether we take a large group of friends and

Once the Phelps family realized this was a tradition they would be doing for years to come, their kids designed colorful covers and created their own family Christmas caroling books.

extended family, or a handful, it is always a highlight.

We usually visit different wards at a local hospital. Some years, the pediatric unit is full of kids who are sick and can't go home for Christmas, or the oncology unit is full of people who don't know if they will live to see another Christmas. Some years, we find that the hospi-

tal is quite empty and we aren't really sure who is listening . . . or maybe people are listening but can't come out of their rooms. Yet even when we end up singing just to the hospital staff, they love it . . . and we know it brings them an extra measure of joy to hear Christmas music when they have to be at work instead of celebrating at home with their families.

We often come out of these visits crying and realizing how blessed we are. And we are always happy that we were able to bring some cheer to people. ✳

IVAN PARKER
Jesus, Lord at Thy Birth

My mother and I were talking about Christmas memories a couple of years ago, and she mentioned the cold December day when she went into labor. Yes, I was coming into this world right before Christmas!

That night, as the labor pains grew stronger, my mom began to pray that God would use this child for His glory. Soon she heard carolers standing outside the hospital window singing Christmas songs. One of those songs was "Silent Night." So, literally, I came into this world hearing Christmas music!

Sometimes in my concerts I sing "Silent Night" and other Christmas carols in honor of my mom. She could probably relate to Mary in a special way that year. And although I am pretty sure my "singing" on that day was a very different melody than the angels' song on that first Christmas night, I am thankful that the story of Jesus has been sung to me since day one! ✳

Whether there is a large group or just a handful, the annual caroling outing is the highlight of the Christmas season for the Phelps family.

Go, tell it on the mountain,
Over the hills and everywhere;
Go, tell it on the mountain
That Jesus Christ is born.

JOHN WESLEY WORK JR.
"GO TELL IT ON THE MOUNTAIN"

JOY GARDNER
Christmas Eve in
Bethlehem Square

On a Christmas Eve several years ago, while my husband, Landy, and I were directing the Christ Church Choir, we had the opportunity to sing in Bethlehem Square. Several choirs from around the world had been invited, but we were one of only two Christian choirs. The square was noisy and boisterous, and the crowd had been working itself into a frenzy all day.

There were 10,000 people gathered, and it was clear they were there for a party. No one was paying attention to what was happening on the stage.

The crowd—seemingly unaware of the real meaning of the occasion—was so aggressive that our choir members had to hold hands and push their way through to get to the platform. We were the last choir on the program, scheduled to sing just moments before midnight. Above the fray we began to sing, "O little town of Bethlehem, how still we see thee lie . . ." A hush fell immediately over the crowd, and the people started making their way toward the stage. The entire atmosphere shifted. When we finished, the event coordinator came to Landy and asked him to lead everyone in Christmas carols until midnight.

For those precious moments, we were unified, blanketed by God's presence. Once again, He came into a chaotic world and brought unexplainable peace. ❄

The Christ Church Choir in Bethlehem Square, singing Christ's peace into a chaotic environment.

Songs of the Season

Late on a sleepy, star-spangled night,
those angels peeled back the sky just like you would
tear open a sparkling Christmas present.
Then, with light and joy pouring out of Heaven
like water through a broken dam,
they began to shout and sing.

LARRY LIBBY

MARK LOWRY
Mary, Did You Know?

I was living in Houston, Texas, where I live now. I was born there, and I had moved back around 1984 to an apartment my dad sold me. (It was a one-bedroom place, and he would stay there when he had to do work in Houston.) I had one of those old Macintosh computers, and this is what I wrote "Mary, Did You Know?" on.

My pastor had called and asked if I would write for a Christmas production the church was working on. And in the course of helping with that, I wrote this one section about Mary that said, "I wonder if Mary realized the power and authority she cradled in her arms that first Christmas morning? I wonder if she realized that those little fingers wrapped around hers were the same ones that had scooped out oceans and formed rivers, and that those little lips were the same that spoke the world into existence—and that compressed and compacted into that eight-pound bundle was the fullness of the Godhead? I wonder if she realized that the little child she delivered that first Christmas would one day deliver her on a cross?" And then I wrote, "And when she kissed the little baby, she kissed the cheek of God."

When I wrote those lines, I kept thinking of the idea of delivery and Deliverer. And the enormity of it almost made me shiver.

At some point, that monologue became a lyric. Working on the Christmas program had caused the idea to germinate and the questions to be asked. But later I started to work on it again, and friends made suggestions. One of them suggested the line, "Mary, did you know too much?" which was great.

Over time I tweaked this word and that word, and then, between 1984 and 1991, I sent the

At the taping of A Christmas Homecoming,
Mark Lowry and Buddy Greene had the opportunity to perform together
the beloved song they cowrote: "Mary, Did You Know?"

Photo by Kevin Sims

lyrics to several folks—Babbie Mason and Paul Johnson and others—who all tried to write music to it. But nothing seemed to work. So I kind of gave up on it. It was one of my favorite children, that lyric. I'd always liked it, but it didn't seem as though it would ever go anywhere.

> NOTHING SEEMED TO WORK. SO I KIND OF GAVE UP ON IT. IT WAS ONE OF MY FAVORITE CHILDREN, THAT LYRIC. I'D ALWAYS LIKED IT, BUT IT DIDN'T SEEM AS THOUGH IT WOULD EVER GO ANYWHERE.

And then I gave it to Buddy Greene. I wrote it out on a piece of paper and said, "Dear Buddy, please take this God-inspired lyric that I wrote several years ago, add some beautiful music to it, and make it a money-making hit, in the clutches of the cross. Mark Lowry." I wish I still had that piece of paper!

Buddy took the lyrics home that weekend, thought about them, and picked up a guitar and wrote the music. Called me after thirty minutes of working on it and sang it to me over the phone. And that was that.

To make a long story short, I cornered Brown Bannister at a Gaither show, ran the song past him, and sold it to him just by singing the thing to him there. He tweaked it into the contemporary version that Michael English—who was the first to ever record the song—cut. Don Potter, who played the guitar on Michael's record, was also playing for Kathy Mattea's Christmas record, and he told her about it and she recorded it. And then I heard that Kathleen Battle, an opera singer, had cut it. By word of mouth, people just kept hearing it and record-

ing it. And now there are over four hundred versions of it on iTunes. There's even a disco version! The biggest-selling version has been Clay Aiken's. My favorite version is Gary Chapman's.

But it all started in a little one-bedroom apartment in Texas. It was a fluke, really. I haven't done anything like it since then—although I've tried. I'm working on "Joseph, Did You Know?" "Moses, Did You Know?" and "Jesus, We Know You Knew!" ✳

BUDDY GREENE
Mary, Did You Know?

I'm thankful to have been a cowriter of "Mary, Did You Know?" Thankful to Mark for passing on to me those lyrics he had been guarding for years and then approving of my musical offering. Thankful to all the great artists like Kathy Mattea, Kenny Rogers, Wynonna, Clay Aiken, Kathleen Battle, Christopher Parkening, and The Isaacs who have recorded wonderful versions and made it the popular Christmas song it has become. And thankful to God for "His indescribable gift" that will continue to inspire songs, stories, dances, movies, symphonies, and master works of every kind. ✳

MARY, DID YOU KNOW?

Mary did you know that your baby boy
would one day walk on water?
Mary did you know that your baby boy
would save our sons and daughters?
Did you know that your baby boy
has come to make you new?
This child that you've delivered, will soon
deliver you.

❧

Mary did you know that your baby boy
would give sight to a blind man?
Mary did you know that your baby boy
would calm a storm with his hand?
Did you know that your baby boy
has walked where angels trod?
And when you kiss your little baby,
you have kissed the face of God.

❧

The blind will see, the deaf will hear,
the dead will live again.
The lame will leap, the dumb will speak,
the praises of the lamb—

❧

Mary did you know that your baby boy
is Lord of all creation?
Mary did you know that your baby boy
would one day rule the nations?
Did you know that your baby boy
is heaven's perfect Lamb?
This sleeping child you're holding
is the great I AM.

WORDS BY MARK LOWRY
MUSIC BY BUDDY GREENE

BILL GAITHER
O Little Town of Bethlehem

I believe one of the most solid pieces of theology about "God with us" can be found in the lyric of "O Little Town of Bethlehem."

Whatever we are feeling—good or bad—is intensified at Christmas. Our emotions are strong throughout the year, but they only increase the closer we get to December 25 . . . and for very good reason. It is the time we stop to acknowledge that God has come to where we are; and because of hope, our greatest expectations are intensified. Christmas can be not only glorious but very tough. The writer of this carol captures this intensity of expectations in this line:

The hopes and fears of all the years are met in thee tonight.

The song goes beyond Christ's birth and reminds us that this baby was born to die. And in our own lives, every joy seems to be paid for in the currency of pain, loss, and disappointment. We can tell a brother or sister or friend our inmost thoughts, and they will probably say they understand, and they will probably try to understand. But it is impossible for any human being to truly feel our hopes and fears like Christ does. He understands fully, which is why He had to come—to "move into the neighborhood," as Eugene Peterson has phrased it. He already knows and shares "our infirmities."

This line sums up the very hope we celebrate, at Christmas and every day . . .

O holy Child of Bethlehem, descend to us, we pray;
Cast out our sin, and enter in, be born in us today. ❄

O LITTLE TOWN OF BETHLEHEM

O little town of Bethlehem, how still we see thee lie!
Above thy deep and dreamless sleep the silent stars go by.
Yet in thy dark streets shineth the everlasting Light;
The hopes and fears of all the years are met in thee tonight.

For Christ is born of Mary, and gathered all above;
While mortals sleep, the angels keep their watch of wondering love.
O morning stars together proclaim the holy birth,
And praises sing to God the King, and peace to men on earth!

How silently, how silently, the wondrous Gift is giv'n;
So God imparts to human hearts the blessings of His Heav'n.
No ear may hear His coming, but in this world of sin,
Where meek souls will receive Him still, the dear Christ enters in.

Where children pure and happy pray to the blessed Child,
Where misery cries out to Thee, Son of the mother mild,
Where charity stands watching and faith holds wide the door,
The dark night wakes, the glory breaks, and Christmas comes once more.

O holy Child of Bethlehem, descend to us, we pray;
Cast out our sin and enter in, be born in us today.
We hear the Christmas angels the great glad tidings tell;
O come to us, abide with us, our Lord Emmanuel!

WORDS BY PHILLIPS BROOKS
MUSIC BY LEWIS H. REDNER

Phillips Brooks completed the lyric of "O Little Town of Bethlehem" two years after he took a
horseback journey from Jerusalem to Bethlehem and assisted with a midnight Christmas Eve service.
He once recalled that experience, stating, "I remember standing in the old church in Bethlehem,
close to the spot where Jesus was born, when the whole church was ringing hour after hour
with splendid hymns of praise to God, how again and again it seemed as if
I could hear voices I knew well, telling each other of the wonderful night of the Savior's birth."

Our Favorite Christmas Songs

TANYA GOODMAN-SYKES
I Heard the Bells on Christmas Day

My favorite Christmas song is "I Heard the Bells on Christmas Day" based on the poem by Henry Longfellow. It was written during the Civil War and reflects on the truth that, even in that dark time of great division in our country, there was hope—the hope that Christ gave us—that right will prevail and eventually His peace will come. I'm not very good at singing it—it always makes me cry—but I love to listen to it. ❈

LYNDA RANDLE
Sweet Little Jesus Boy

"**S**weet Little Jesus Boy" is a Negro spiritual that has been passed down through generations, and I've always loved and appreciated the humble lyrics. The songwriter may not have been prolific, but the song is profound! ❄

CHARLOTTE RITCHIE
O Little Town of Bethlehem

I have two favorite Christmas songs. The first one is "The Christmas Song." When I hear that song, I am immediately immersed in the sights, sounds, smells, and feelings of Christmas. The second is "O Little Town of Bethlehem." I love how it sets the scene of the coming of Christ. I especially love the line, "The hopes and fears of all the years are met in thee tonight." It reminds us that, yes, Christ came to redeem us, but also to be involved in the details of our lives. ❄

Hopes and fears make up a great part of our days. The birth of Christ our Redeemer is miraculous, and the fact that all of our hopes and fears can be met in Him is truly amazing!

REBECCA ISAACS BOWMAN
Labor of Love

My favorite Christmas song is "Labor of Love" by Andrew Peterson. The song paints the picture of what it must have really been like the night Jesus was born. It does not glamorize Christmas, but instead allows us to feel compassion for Mary and the humble night of our Lord's birth. ❄

Years after giving her heart to Jesus on Christmas, Becky still cherishes this season and, along with her husband, John, is passing along the story of Jesus to her own kids.

ANDY ANDREWS
Labor of Love

I love all Christmas music, and the boys and I would play Christmas music 365 days a year if Mom would let us. For a long time I've said "Mary, Did You Know?" is my favorite Christmas song—partially because Mark Lowry will probably be reading this and he is a good friend of mine, and partially because it's true. But also at the top I have to add "Labor of Love" sung by the Isaacs. That song ranks with "Mary, Did You Know?" in the blew-me-away category. ❄

It was a labor of pain
It was a cold sky above
But for the girl on the ground in the dark
With every beat of her beautiful heart
It was a labor of love

ANDREW PETERSON
"LABOR OF LOVE"

LUANN BURGER
Mary, Did You Know?

"Mary, Did You Know?" has become my most meaningful Christmas song in recent years. I had always enjoyed hearing it, but it seems like after the passing of my eighteen-year-old son Gary Jr., it became much more significant. Being able to relate in some small way to Mary, her dreams for her son, and his unanticipated early death makes it an endearing song for me.

During my last years of traveling with Anthony on the Gaither Homecoming tour, the Christmas concerts were some of my favorites. Each night, it was wonderful to hear Mark deliver those powerful words, all the while feeling a poignant reminder of my loss and how Mary must have felt. ❄

Hearing
CHRISTMAS
~ *Calvin Miller* ~

But all the music of the season
isn't grand, choral majesty.
Consider the simplicity of a
grandmother singing.
She has grown older now, and for her,
the higher notes have left the upper clef
and resolved themselves in
a gorgeous, gravelly alto.
Still, something lovely is birthed in
the music of all those who
have long sung, and have believed
for as long as they have sung.
Those who, Christmas by Christmas,
were accompanied
by a luminous web of melodies—
some born of earth,
some born in church,
but all born in faith.
The ear is given then to the heart.
Grandma is singing,
and the whole world is called alive,
her melody the best part of the music that
breaks out around us.

Continued on page 62

Photo by Russ Harrington

JASON CRABB
Joseph

I've been singing a song called "Joseph" that was written from his perspective. It's a newer song, and though I was one of the first artists to record it, it's going to be around for a while! It explains some ideas about what Joseph must have felt like when all of this happened, when all of it came down.

One of the verses says, "Did you want to pack your tools and head off to someplace where nobody was saying, 'There goes Mary's fool'?" And then another part speaks of how it must have felt to know that God trusted him to take care of Mary and Himself. Man, what a line that is! It's just a well-written song. ❄

SHERI EASTER
The Greatest Gift of All

Jeff and I got engaged on December 21, 1984. He had cued the Kenny Rogers and Dolly Parton song "The Greatest Gift of All" and had the song playing while he presented me with my engagement ring. That song was so special to us that we began singing it each year in concert. Then we finally had the opportunity to record it on our first Christmas project. We sang it while we held each other's hands—performing it on the Homecoming Christmas in South Africa special while our third child, who was only eight weeks old at the time, was at home with our two older children. Last Christmas our oldest got married and chose to have this song played while we lit the unity candles as a family. ❄

SONYA ISAACS-YEARY
Rockin' Around the Christmas Tree

I would have to say that my all-time favorite Christmas songs are "The Christmas Song" and Brenda Lee's "Rockin' Around the Christmas Tree." It's just not Christmas to me till I hear both of these songs! "The Christmas Song" captures all the sensations of the holiday in such a beautiful, romantic way, and "Rockin' Around the Christmas Tree" just makes me want to sing and smile and shop! I love them both. ❄

Sonya and Jimmy rocking around their own Christmas tree—or at least smiling next to it.

"I'll be home for Christmas . . . you can count on me!"
KIM GANNON, WALTER KENT, AND BUCK RAM

MICHAEL ENGLISH
I'll Be Home for Christmas

I would say our most meaningful Christmas song is "I'll Be Home for Christmas," because in the past I was always on the road. But I have promised Marcie and Bella that I will always be there for Christmas with my family. ❄

RUSS TAFF
White Christmas

When I was growing up in the small Pentecostal church that my father pastored, I was taught that listening to any music other than gospel was a sin. We were also not allowed to watch TV, listen to the radio, or read a newspaper because all of that was considered to be "partaking of the world." The only entertainment that we could enjoy without being worried about losing our salvation was Mama's record collection. She had so many albums—The Statesmen Quartet, Happy Goodmans, Mahalia Jackson, Clara Ward.

The family groups, quartets, and soloists had simple arrangements with pretty basic accompaniment, but they sang with so much passion! I have such clear memories of lying stretched out on the floor with my head positioned between the two speakers of Mom's record player, eyes closed, tears running down my cheeks, drinking that music in. Those years formed my own singing style and instilled in me a deep love for gospel music.

> I WAS THIRTEEN YEARS OLD WHEN I WAS TOLD THAT MY BROTHER MARVIN HAD BEEN DRAFTED INTO THE ARMY AND WOULD SOON BE ON HIS WAY TO VIETNAM.

I was thirteen years old when I was told that my brother Marvin had been drafted into the army and would soon be on his way to Vietnam. Shortly before he shipped out, Marvin broke all tradition (and the Taff family rules) and went out and bought a SECULAR

record! He walked in the door of our little house and boldly put it on Mom's record player and called me in to listen. It was Bing Crosby's "White Christmas," with the Andrews Sisters singing backup. My ears were suddenly filled with the most beautiful, lush musical arrangements and intricate vocals I had ever heard. I immediately began trying to figure out those chords on my guitar, and when I managed to pick out the melody, I started singing along with Bing—and Mom, who was a wonderful singer, actually joined in, singing harmony to my vocals! I couldn't believe it! When I looked up from my guitar in shock, the expression on her face seemed to say, "We shouldn't be doing this . . . but isn't it beautiful?"

All these years later, ol' Bing's Christmas CD is the first one I play every holiday season; and as soon as I hear those opening notes of Irving Berlin's "White Christmas," I get a warm smile on my face. It always brings me back to that very first time, when even my holy-rolling mom couldn't resist the sound of that glorious, forbidden music. ❋

WOODY WRIGHT
Little Drummer Boy

Growing up in the '70s, music was the focal point of my life. (My grades in school aptly confirmed that fact.) So for at least four years, in the weeks before Christmas, I decorated the old upright piano in my bedroom with large, colored Christmas lights. With the sound of everything from the Oak Ridge Boys' "Street Gospel" to Elton John's "Tumbleweed Connection" blaring through the Panasonic stereo speakers, the old upright was rocking with holiday cheer!

My dad and I played guitars together. He helped me to learn songs, and we would play along with the country music television programs on Saturdays: Flatt and Scruggs, the Wilburn Brothers, Porter Waggoner, and others who had weekly programs that aired in Knoxville. One year, a lady from a church we had attended asked if I would sing a special song in the Christmas program. I was about seven or eight years old. They made a prop drum for me, and I sang "Little Drummer Boy."

After that program, our family began to attend the church regularly. I sang occasionally with two other young fellows at church, and a few years later I sang in the youth choir. Eventually, I even started a teenage singing group. We recorded several albums and traveled around the South.

For obvious reasons, "Little Drummer Boy" is a song I still sing at Christmas and is one of the most special of Christmas songs to me. ❋

ANN DOWNING
Silent Night

A favorite Christmas carol for me is "Silent Night," particularly because it was my mama's favorite.

The last Christmas she was with us, she was in a nursing home. Mama hadn't sung very much in years—she felt her voice wasn't up to it. I always begged her to sing with us at Christmas, but she would usually decline, even though I thought her crystal-clear soprano was the most beautiful sound I'd ever heard.

But that year was different. Little did we know

Ladye Love and Reggie Smith and their son, Bret, get dressed up to attend the annual Christmas Eve candlelight service, which always ends with "Silent Night."

that this was to be her last Christmas on earth. We gathered around the bed in her room, joined hands to sing "her favorite," and she joined in! How thrilling to hear that sweet, high voice singing along once more!

God left me a beautiful memory. It was almost as if she was singing from both places—here and there! ❋

LADYE LOVE SMITH
O Holy Night

I have two meaningful Christmas songs. One is "Silent Night," because I first sang it in a Christmas Eve service and sang a verse in German. The other is "O Holy Night," because every year my godmother and mentor would sing it at our church. My favorite line from it is, "Surely He taught us to love one another. His law is love and His gospel is peace." ❋

BUDDY GREENE
Joy to the World

I'm always glad to hear the first Christmas song on the radio or in department stores, even as early as Thanksgiving. Christmas music, especially the traditional variety, is about all I listen to until the season's over. I love going to church during Advent, playing at worship services and Christmas concerts, and participating in various seasonal events.

I have so many favorites—"Joy to the World," "In the Bleak Midwinter," "The Christmas Song," "What Child Is This?," "What a Wonderful World," etc. But the most meaningful are the ones like "Joy to the World" that preach the kingdom.

I also enjoy the old chestnuts. One of my earliest memories is listening to Perry Como's Christmas album. It was magical hearing songs like "The Night Before Christmas," "Adeste Fideles," and "Rudolph the Red-Nosed Reindeer." They transported me instantly to this place of eager anticipation that didn't let up until Christmas morning. ✽

He Started *the* Whole World Singing

GLORIA GAITHER
The Story Behind the Song

New York at Christmas is unlike any other place on earth—a candy store for the senses. Already uniquely diverse and stimulating, at Christmastime the city assaults you with lights, smells, and sounds at every turn. Hot dog vendors, pretzel makers, and chestnut roasters send aromas into the chilly air. Speakers flood the street with music from the doorway of every restaurant and store. The sides of skyscrapers illuminate the skyline with all symbols of the season painted in colored lights. The designer-arranged windows of huge department stores are so amazing that people linc up to take pictures of them. At Rockefeller Center, the world-famous Christmas tree, sparkling with thousands of lights and ornaments, towers over the skaters who glide over the ice-covered square flanked with enormous golden angels.

A horse-drawn carriage ride at night through Central Park with someone you love is magical enough, but should the snow start to fall while you're wrapped cozy and warm in coats and lap blankets, you'll have the chance to experience one of the most romantic hours of your life.

Because our anniversary falls on December 22nd, Bill and I have celebrated a few times in New York. We love to eat in our favorite restaurants, uninterrupted by phones, and then take in a great play or musical. Afterward, we walk around Manhattan and Times Square just like a couple of kids from some small, country town in the Midwest—which we are!

One night at Christmas, we were eating in the grand old German restaurant called Luchow's. The place was decorated with ancient ornaments and garlands that looked as if they had actually come from Germany years before and had been some family's treasure.

An aging polka band used to play there then, and people who knew how to polka got up to dance. But this was Christmas, so the band played Christmas carols to people's request, and as they played, guests began to sing along. We couldn't help but join in. There we were in the middle of the city with a reputation for being secular and politically correct, singing with folks

> THERE WE WERE IN THE MIDDLE OF THE CITY WITH A REPUTATION FOR BEING SECULAR AND POLITICALLY CORRECT, SINGING WITH FOLKS WE'D NEVER MET: "JOY TO THE WORLD, THE LORD IS COME! LET EARTH RECEIVE HER KING . . ."

we'd never met: "Joy to the world, the Lord is come! Let earth receive her King . . ."

One after another, those diners requested their favorites; and around these well-worn songs, instant community was created. People grinned at each other as the parts were added, and sometimes they applauded when the song was over.

After the singing subsided and the band went back to playing traditional German pieces, Bill looked at me and said, "Well, at least He got everyone singing, didn't He?"

The next night, we had tickets to the Radio City Music Hall Christmas show. This is always an incredible production, and the performance was spectacular. From the Sugar Plum Fairy to Frosty the Snowman and Rudolph the Red-Nosed Reindeer, everything to delight a child appeared bigger than life. The dramatization of Virginia's letter to Santa and the classic, "Yes, Virginia, There Is a Santa Claus" response from the *New York Times* left even the hardest of hearts wishing every child had someone to be Santa for them.

The procession choreography of the famous Rockettes dancing the "March of the Toy Soldiers" brought the entire audience to its feet in thunderous applause. Then the curtain closed and a whole different atmosphere was created. A strong voice began to read the Christmas story from the second chapter of Luke. When the curtain reopened, the huge stage was a craggy hillside, and the characters in the real story of Christmas began to enter the scene: Mary and Joseph, the infant Jesus, shepherds with their sheep and goats, animals that belonged in the stable, and the donkey

Hearing CHRISTMAS

~ *Calvin Miller* ~

Sound is the gift; listening is the discipline.

The eardrum is the receptor of all we feel.

For God sometimes sets aside

the anthems of the angels

And sings in the ordinary lyrics of

doorbells and sleigh bells

And simmering tones of bright, brassy

kettles filled with turkey and noodles.

And yes, the sweet sound of the choir

at our Christmas Eve service.

And of course, as sweet as all of them rejoicing

in a single voice

is the aged testament of my

grandmother singing

her husky allegiance to the babe in the manger,

"I love Thee, Lord Jesus, look down from the sky

And stay by my cradle till morning is nigh."

that had made the trip to Bethlehem all came to the hilltop shelter. Along the side of the great auditorium came the camels too, and Oriental kings with their lavish array, bowing at last before the baby monarch, offering gifts to honor His birth.

Then a screen slowly lowered, and on it, scrolling down line-by-line, was the wonderful piece we have come to know as "One Solitary Life." Awe and wonder had reduced the audience to total silence at the panorama before us. No one moved as the voice finished the last lines . . .

> *All the armies that ever marched,*
> *all the navies that were ever built;*
> *all the parliaments that ever sat*
> *and all the kings that ever reigned,*
> *have not affected the life of man upon this earth*
> *as powerfully as has that one solitary life.**

The silence remained.

When Bill and I got home, we talked about the song of Jesus—how His coming to earth gave us back the Song that had been silent for so long through the centuries. Bill began writing the music for the chorus to "He Started the Whole World Singing." A few months later, we began writing a musi-

cal that was born of these experiences. As I explored the biblical story of the departure and return of the glory that was present in the beginning when man and God walked together and found delight in each other, I discovered that the quaint old word *glory* meant eternal, and that it infused everything—all of life—before sin entered the picture. And during those long years after the glory departed and the song died, God chose a people and gave them the promise that one day the glory would return and life would have a song. He gave them the law as a gift to "save the frame" for the promised glory, and He instructed His people to keep alive the story of when God walked and talked with man and woman by telling it to their children until God's plan would be made perfect again.

No wonder the angels sang that night to the shepherds: "Glory! Glory to the highest degree! This night is born to you a Savior which is Christ the Lord!"

What they sang that night was not a song; it was the Song. The Song had returned to the world! The Song had returned to our lives! And all over the world to this day, the Song goes on. The Eternal has infused our days. The Glory has returned to our lives. And the song still echoes in the hearts of those who allow it to invade their lives—even in the streets of New York. ❄

Excerpted from *He Started the Whole World Singing* by Gloria Gaither (New York: FaithWords/Hachette Book Group, 2004).
*Dr. James Allan Francis, "One Solitary Life, The Real Jesus and Other Sermons" (Phildelphia, PA: Judson Press, 1926).

Come On, Ring Those Bells

Joy bells are ringing
Christmas is bringing
Tidings of Jesus' birth.
Candles are gleaming
Gladness is streaming
Out over all the earth.

Nils Frykman and W. Theodor Söderberg
"Joy Bells Are Ringing"

SOLVEIG LEITHAUG
Ringing in Hope

On Christmas Eve in Norway, our family would always step outside on the patio—even in freezing temperatures (if we were lucky, it was snowing)—in time to hear the church bells ringing in Christmas

at 5 p.m. sharp. Then we would gather at the dinner table where Dad would read the Christmas story, followed by us singing a verse of a carol (sometimes it was "Silent Night"). Being a musical family, it was the norm that we would all try to hunt for the harmony part that no one else had already grabbed, making our own little three- or four-part impromptu chorus in time for a lengthy "Amen" at least! Another fond memory is walking around the Christmas tree, holding hands with my siblings, parents, in-laws, nephews, and nieces, while singing carols.

Although Christmas with family is great, among my most sacred memories is singing in jails or prisons in the Advent season. The brokenness, humility, and receptivity I have been met with have brought about some of the most beautiful times I have ever experienced. For several years while living in Colorado, I assisted with

Somewhere along the way, they decided to call me "Mom"—and they still do. When Mario, who is now a songwriter and worship leader, got married to his lovely Crystal a couple of years ago, my children were in the wedding as flower girl, ring bearer, and usher. Now Mario is teaching his little son Jonathan Jude to call me "Grandma." Though I admit this is flattering, I am not so sure I am ready for this title just yet!

One might argue about the validity of celebrating Christmas in these war-torn, conflicting, and challenging times. But Henry Wadsworth Longfellow's words in "I Heard the Bells on Christmas Day"—written in 1863 after he was recently widowed and his son had been gravely injured in war—still ring strong and true with a much-needed message of peace and hope, even for today. ❆

I heard the bells on Christmas day
Their old familiar carols play,
And wild and sweet the words repeat
Of peace on earth, good will to men.

I thought how, as the day had come,
The belfries of all Christendom
Had rolled along the unbroken song
Of peace on earth, good will to men.

And in despair I bowed my head:
"There is no peace on earth," I said,
"For hate is strong and mocks the song
Of peace on earth, good will to men."

Then pealed the bells more loud and deep:
"God is not dead, nor doth he sleep;
The wrong shall fail, the right prevail,
With peace on earth, good will to men."

HENRY WADSWORTH LONGFELLOW
"I HEARD THE BELLS ON CHRISTMAS DAY"

facilitating outreaches and special events for the homeless and needy. My children also helped out, and Christmas was a time that we tried to make extra-special.

I am blessed to still have frequent contact with several of the young men and women who were once living on the streets when we first met them, like Mario, Tonya, and Aaron. Over time, and through the time, resources, and care that many people invested in their lives, these young people have managed to turn their lives around.

TANYA GOODMAN-SYKES
Sleigh Bells Ring!

When I was nine or ten years old, I was beginning to doubt whether good ol' Santa really existed, and this troubled my dad [Rusty Goodman] to no end. My dad was a big kid when it came to Christmas—I believe he would have started decorating for the holiday around Labor Day if my mom had let him! So when he grew really concerned that the wonder of St. Nick was starting to wane, he sprang into action.

On Christmas Eve, our family went to Uncle Howard and Aunt Vestal's house to celebrate with a big family meal and lots of presents. My dad had made "special arrangements" for Santa to visit our house just before we returned home for the evening. As we opened the front door, my sister and I heard jingle bells and a "ho, ho, ho" coming from the far end of the house. We raced to the other room to find the window open and the curtains flying in the breeze. We were overcome with excitement and ran out into the yard where we found lots of reindeer tracks.

Whatever doubts I had were put to flight that night! My sister and I were so amped up, I don't think we slept a wink. That's probably why the jingling of sleigh bells is one of my favorite sounds of the season. To this day when I hear them, I can close my eyes and be transported back to that moment. It makes me smile to think about the planning that my dad put into that evening—I'm sure he had to really work with Santa to schedule that whole thing! ❄

When Christmas bells are swinging above the fields of snow,
we hear sweet voices ringing from lands of long ago,
and etched on vacant places are half-forgotten faces
of friends we used to cherish, and loves we used to know.

ELLA WHEELER WILCOX
"CHRISTMAS FANCIES"

The Music *of* Laughter

KARLYE HOPPER
Laughter

The crisp crunch of soft, quiet snow beneath our boots; biting clashes of delicate glass ornaments meeting wooden floor with a shatter; the playfully nagging jingles, dinging, and honking of every mildly inhabited area . . . What does it sound like? Festivities. Holiday. Oh, but laughter—the one honest, true sound of joy. Laughter is the sound of Christmas.

Joking around and poking innocent fun: it's what fuels my day. Being a teenage girl in a world where every-

Karlye Hopper . . .
just being her fun, wonderful self at home.

one tries so hard to be taken seriously, I personally would much rather laugh. Lucky for me, I have a family that enjoys it all the same—a family that wouldn't allow the sun to either rise or set without a little bit of humor. Even the Bible says that a merry heart does good like a medicine, so why wouldn't God Himself want His Son's celebratory day—which to some is a reminder of the estranged and the hurting—to be filled with His "medicine"?

The Hopper family is never short on laughter, and pictured here is Karlye with her funny little sister, Lexy, who is all dressed up as Mrs. Claus.

Whether it is the grimace of frustration over burnt pies, the mismatched loafers that managed to make their way through gift wrapping and reopening, or the subtle moment of nostalgia where all of the ghastly stories of Christmases past come flooding back and then sink into a quiet chuckle, you must ask, did any of those things ever really matter? Of course not. The mess-ups and *faux pas* were all little trickles of joy for you to feel, memories for you to keep, and reasons for you to laugh . . . ❋

WOODY WRIGHT
Laughing All the Way

For the past seven years, the weeks of December prior to Christmas have found me mostly in airports, rental cars, and hotels. Another good portion of time has been spent setting up and tearing down gear and product tables. Seems like the smallest portion of time is spent actually doing concerts. Stephen Hill and I have enjoyed our "Spirit of Christmas" concert tour in dozens of states, along with shows in Norway, Sweden, the Netherlands, and Canada. Though our program evolves each year, there are always healthy portions of Christmas standards and carols along with original compositions and HUMOR!

We discovered early on that the Christmas season is very difficult for many people. I can't tell you how many times folks have come up after concerts to not only say thanks for the music, but also for the chance to laugh. Broken families, lost loved ones, harsh memories, financial distress, depression, and hopelessness often invade what should be the most joyous time of year. I can relate to the emotional upheaval that the holidays can bring, because at different stages of life, I have spent Christmas seasons enduring many of those hardships myself.

So it is especially heartwarming for me when someone comes up after a concert, smiling through tears, to thank me for sharing the story, the hope, the humor, and the spirit of Christmas! It is so fitting that sharing our Christmas program would bring hope where there seems to be little. It

Woody and Vonnie

is a tiny representation of the hope that Christ—the Word—brought to a hopeless world by stooping down to our level to become flesh and dwell among us.

There is power in the true Spirit of Christmas. I believe that is why doors keep opening for Stephen and me to do twenty or more concerts each year. I also believe that as long as we continue to spread that Spirit, we will continue to encourage folks to dash through the snow, laughing all the way! ❄

> *Dashing through the snow*
> *In a one-horse open sleigh*
> *O'er the fields we go*
> *Laughing all the way!*
>
> James Lord Pierpont
> "Jingle Bells"

GORDON MOTE
"Listening" to the Lights

There is just something about the sound of a choir singing certain Christmas songs! It takes me back to Christmases when my brother and I were kids. My mom and daddy taught us early on what Christmas really means. I grew up singing in choirs and understanding how those songs tell the real story of Christmas, so the music triggers years of happy memories.

Now Mom comes and spends Christmas at our house, and while we have kept some of the traditions I grew up with, we as a family have also started our own traditions with our kids. It's great to have Mom be a part of our traditions after she created so many great memories for me through the years.

Our family started one tradition several years ago that we call "Shakes and Lights." We go out and get our favorite milkshakes, and then ride around to look at Christmas lights while we slurp our shakes. Though I can't see the lights, I enjoy the milkshake and, most of all, I love hearing Kimberly and the kids react to all they are seeing. This has become one of our favorite family traditions . . . where they look, and I listen. ❄

The Mote family loves driving around and enjoying their "Lights and Shakes" tradition, then they come home to their own beautifully lit home!

Family Harmony

DAVID & LORI PHELPS
A Family Christmas Eve Service

Last year our schedules were especially crazy in December, so we couldn't go caroling until Christmas Eve night. By the time we were finished with that, it was getting too late to make it to a Christmas Eve service, so we decided to have our own family Christmas Eve service around the piano in our living room. In addition to our immediate family, David's parents were there, along with his sister and her family and some close

The Phelps family's own impromptu Christmas Eve service!

friends. David played the piano; our oldest son, Grant, played guitar; and the rest of us sang from our family songbooks that the kids had created. Our brother-in-law reminded us of some very important historical events leading up to Jesus' birth, such as the prophecy in Daniel , and then David's dad read the Christmas story. It was wonderful! We all agreed it might have been the best Christmas Eve service any of us could remember. ❋

TANYA GOODMAN-SYKES
Dad's Last Christmas Around the Piano

These photos were taken in 1989, the last Christmas that my dad was alive. After our family moved to Nashville, we spent lots of Christmas Eves with our cousins, the Hemphills. LaBreeska is a wonderful hostess who always prepared a delicious meal, and we would play games and sing around the piano. These were taken in their home, and they're quite a treasure to me. They are the last holiday photos I have of my dad and some of his siblings together. ❋

Howard Goodman (at piano), Gussie Rudd (sister, in fur hat), Vestal Goodman (in red and black top), Stella Messer (sister, in gray top), Rusty Goodman (my dad, seated in sweatshirt), LaBreeska Hemphill (in black and silver pantsuit).

KIM HOPPER
Christmas Eve at Grandmother Snow's

One tradition that I love happens at my Grandmother Snow's house on Christmas Eve. Granny lives in a very small home, and our large (and growing) family consumes the place. The space is so limited that most of us sit on the floor, stand along the walls, or even listen to what's happening from the kitchen. We always start with one of the men reading the true Christmas story, followed by a time of thanking God for His blessings and the small miracles He has done in our individual lives within the past year.

Next comes the music. I'm so grateful for the musical family from which I come; you can distinguish the harmonies as we blend our voices and sing those familiar Christmas hymns. By this time, most of us are shedding a few tears of sentimentality, and someone always remarks on how marvelous God's gift to the world is and forever will be. Later, we tear into the gifts and find ourselves in a home filled with thank yous, I love yous, hugs, and kisses. This is a time that we all cherish and look forward to again in 364 days! ❊

BILL GAITHER
Singing Mom Home

I will forever remember my mother's last Christmas. On Christmas Eve we all gathered at Mom and Dad's house—grown kids, grandkids, and great-grandkids. My son, Benjy, son-in-law Barry, and grandson Will were playing guitars, and we were all singing, as we often do when we get together. The little ones were dancing around to the music, having fun. In the middle of all the celebrating, Mother—whose memory had been slipping—got up two or three times and said, "George, we ought to get home . . ."

"We are home!" my father reminded her. She laughed, and the kids teased, and we all went back to singing. She would tap her fingers to the beat of the music—I can still see her fingers strumming as we sang.

That Christmas Eve, in the middle of the night, she had a stroke and died. But her last night on earth had been filled with laughter and singing. I can't help but think that she was right when she said, "George, we ought to go home." Right then, in the middle of the music and the laughter and the feasting and the joy, *we ought to go home*! It doesn't get any better than that! Mom went from one celebration to another, singing and tapping her fingers to the rhythm of life all the way! ❊

Lela Gaither, sitting by the fire.

Hearing Him *in the* Silence

EMILY SUTHERLAND
Sounds of Silence

In those rare, silent moments—maybe late at night after everyone is settled into bed, or early in the morning before the hum of Christmas busyness begins—there is possibly no music in the world more beautiful than that holiday silence. To stop and allow the tension in your shoulders to release, to breathe deeply and simply listen. It is amazing how full the silence can be . . . full of insight, beauty, peace, and often, full of Christmas surprise . . . full of Him and brimming with the very Reason we celebrate.

Christmas, with all its fanfare, is rich in sensory experiences. Silence is that one, undemanding, often-overlooked opportunity to hear something not everyone else will take the time to hear. Silence is a veritable hidden treasure of life-changing moments through which we can process the story, the music, the beauty, the experiences of Christmas, and let our hearts absorb their significance. ❉

Hear Him in the Silence
Listen to the joy—
The music of celebration.
Then listen to the silence—
The music of contemplation.

Listen first with your ears
Full with the season's hymns;
Then listen with your heart . . .
Full with Him.

EMILY SUTHERLAND
"HEAR HIM IN THE SILENCE"

SILENT COMES THE JOY

Silent comes the joy
Without proud announcement
Like the hint of dawn
Is whispered to the night
So then without warning
Morning breaks victorious
Extravagant and glorious
Heralding the day

❧

Silent comes the joy
Delivered to a manger
In the quiet night
Of stable and the world
A world in need of angels
And visions of life's meaning
To reinstate the dreaming
That sin had torn away

❧

Silent comes the joy
Like a spring erupting
Unseen in the desert
Then carving out a stream
Coursing down the mountain
Soon a torrent swelling
Jubilantly telling
The pow'r of the unseen

GLORIA GAITHER, WILLIAM J. GAITHER,
AND JEFF KENNEDY

© 1988 Gaither Music Company / Hanna Street Music

Silent Night, Holy Night

"For unto us a child is born, to us a son is given, and the government will be upon his shoulders. And he will be called Wonderful Counselor, Mighty God, Everlasting Father, Prince of Peace." —Isaiah 9:6

SILENT NIGHT, HOLY NIGHT

"Silent Night" began as a poem written in German by an Austrian priest named Joseph Mohr in 1816. The story is told that on Christmas Eve in 1818, in the tiny alpine village of Oberndorf, the organ at St. Nicholas Church broke and could not be played at the midnight Mass. Father Mohr gave his poem (called "Stille Nacht" because it was written in German) to a friend named Franz Xavier Gruber, who composed the melody to be played on a guitar in time for midnight Mass.

Not until 1859 was "Stille Nacht" translated into English as we commonly sing it today. The English version was published by John Freeman Young, second bishop of the Episcopal dioceses of Florida, and since that time, it has become one of the most popular Christmas songs of all time.

Perhaps the world has a special affinity for this song because it points us to the one thing most of us spend every other day of the year searching for: heavenly peace.

Silent night, holy night
All is calm, all is bright
Round yon virgin mother and Child
Holy infant so tender and mild
Sleep in heavenly peace
Sleep in heavenly peace

Silent night, holy night
Shepherds quake at the sight
Glories stream from heaven afar
Heavenly hosts sing Alleluia
Christ the Saviour is born
Christ the Saviour is born

Silent night, holy night
Son of God, Love's pure light
Radiant beams from Thy holy face
With the dawn of redeeming grace
Jesus, Lord, at Thy birth
Jesus, Lord, at Thy birth

WORDS BY JOSEPH MOHR
MUSIC BY FRANZ XAVIER GRUBER

Touching
CHRISTMAS

❋ ❋ ❋

What a wild circus of textures Christmas is!
Come, let's "feel our way"
around the glories of this tactile celebration!

First, feel the soft skin of a baby, who is God-made-most-touchable for us who "were afar off."

Tenderly embrace a child, to honor Him who was Love in a baby blanket . . . held in human arms.

Touch the rough texture of a well-worn wooden manger and the prickly straw that fills it.

Touch the moist noses of the cows and horses that stand nearby, curious.

Feel the night air. Then embrace the celebration that has gradually come to surround this "most touchable" occasion. Feel the needles and boughs of the evergreen tree, which announces that because of Jesus we shall always live!

Touch the snow that covers the ground and remember the "covering"—the atonement—that makes us "whiter than snow" in the eyes of God.

Touch the red berries on the branches we gather and put in all sorts of containers, remembering that the child we celebrate would one day shed His blood so that its life-giving qualities could fill us all, no matter the shape, size, or condition of our vessels.

Touch the lights as they burn warm. String them everywhere. Light the streets and the houses, the cathedrals and the back streets, for the chill of death has been replaced by warmth and light.

Touch your children, your neighbors—your community—with reconciliation. Take someone a warm cake; extend a warm handshake; offer the thawing warmth of forgiveness.

Hold and ring the gold and silver bells. Ring out the news that the Creator of the galaxies has touched us. Yes, ring the bells and pass on the good news! Touch someone else. We are not alone!

Gloria Gaither

FEELING THE
Glory
~ *Calvin Miller* ~

For some, Christmas may at first seem
too touchy-feely.
But touching is the high point of the season.
God literally touched earth at Bethlehem
through a Jewish baby who
presented even us Gentiles with eternity—
the touch of eternal grace for us all.

❦

Tenderly embrace a child, and you will have
accessed the long-ago estate of God,
come to our needy race as Love
bundled in a blanket, held in Mary's arms.

❦

Why would God ever want to become a baby?
Because God wanted to
introduce Himself in such a way
that none of us would be afraid of Him:
with hands so chubby,
they had never held a weapon;
with eyes so bright with innocence,
they had never looked on sin—
and never would;
with feet so tender,
they would never march to any hymn of hate.
Who could fear a God, cooing in a cradle?

Continued on page 85

HANDMADE MEMORIES

And the Grinch, with his Grinch-feet ice cold in the snow,
stood puzzling and puzzling, how could it be so?
It came without ribbons. It came without tags.
It came without packages, boxes or bags.
And he puzzled and puzzled 'till his puzzler was sore.
Then the Grinch thought of something he hadn't before.
What if Christmas, he thought, doesn't come from a store?
What if Christmas, perhaps, means a little bit more?

DR. SEUSS
THE GRINCH WHO STOLE CHRISTMAS

 # TANYA GOODMAN-SYKES
Stringing Garland

One year the girls and I had watched some Christmas movie—I don't recall which one—and the family in the movie
had popcorn garland on their tree. My girls were totally intrigued
by it and were itching to string popcorn for our tree. The next day
I popped a TON of popcorn, gathered some children's sewing
needles and string, and we went to work. About a half an hour

in, their enthusiasm evaporated. Needless to say, I ended up stringing popcorn half the night! But, they did love it when we wound it around the tree . . . and it smelled WONDERFUL! ❋

JOYCE MARTIN
Simple Beauty

When I was in the second grade, we lived in a little house in rural Arkansas that didn't have electricity. Money was tight, and at Christmas we didn't buy fancy, store-bought Christmas decorations—we made our own.

Most of the time we would get a cypress tree from our woods. We would go outside and collect sweet-gum balls and cover them with tin foil to make Christmas balls. We used colored construction paper to make paper chains for garland, and we made snowmen out of white construction paper circles and glued little black paper hats on them. We would put school pictures on canning lids, and some years we would string popcorn that we had popped over the fireplace in an old-fashioned, square popcorn popper.

It never quite seemed right for Christmas trees to blink and shine. To this day, when I see homemade ornaments, it takes me back and makes me smile. ❋

SONYA ISAACS-YEARY
Charlie Brown Tree

My earliest Christmas memory takes me back to when I was a little girl. Dad had broken his back that year on the job and wasn't able to work. We couldn't afford a nice tree, or decorations, or very many presents, so he went into the woods behind our house and found the only tree he could that even resembled a Christmas tree. I remember Becky, Ben, and myself cutting construction paper into different shapes and gluing on glitter and pictures of ourselves. I remember stringing macaroni noodles onto yarn to make our own garland; and I remember, more than anything, how much love we all felt for each other that year as we held hands in front of our "Charlie Brown Christmas tree" and thanked God for all that we did have. Especially each other. ❋

Gifts . . . Love You *can* Hold *in* Your Hands

Touching Christmas

Remember
This December,
That love weighs more than gold!

JOSEPHINE DODGE DASKAM BACON

CHARLOTTE RITCHIE
A Mother's Sacrifice

When I was about eight, the gift to have was a Cabbage Patch Kid. The dolls were such a hot item that people would get into fights over them. It was pure craziness! So like every other girl my age, a Cabbage Patch Kid was at the top of my list. However, I told myself not to be too disappointed if I didn't get one.

When Christmas morning came, I didn't get one—I got two! For weeks my mom had been searching for this doll, even going without sleep to try and fulfill my Christmas wish. It is one of my favorite memories of Christmas, not just because I got exactly what I wanted, but because it showed me that my mom loved me so much that she was willing to sacrifice sleep to make me smile. ❋

JASON CRABB
A Country Boy's Dream Come True

When I was a kid—I can't remember how old I was, maybe five or six years old—I wanted a BB gun really badly . . . because I lived in the country! We didn't have a whole

lot of money, and sometimes we did without, so I knew it was kind of a stretch.

So on Christmas, all the kids opened up everything . . . and the gun just wasn't there. I was excited about what I got, but I was really hoping for that BB gun. Then I saw this little bitty package, and I'll never forget it: it was round, and it was wrapped up. I opened it, and it was BBs! When I turned around, my parents had the gun in their arms, and they were giving it to me!

I'll never forget that. Now that I have kids, when they get the one thing that they are all gung-ho about, it kind of makes me go back to that moment. ❋

"Next to me in the
blackness lay my
oiled blue steel beauty.
The greatest Christmas gift
I had ever received,
or would ever receive. Gradually,
I drifted off to sleep, pranging ducks on the wing
and getting off spectacular hip shots."

RALPHIE IN *A CHRISTMAS STORY*

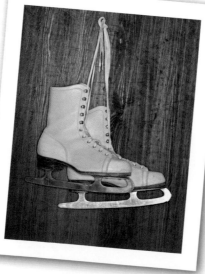

SOLVEIG LEITHAUG
White Figure Skates

Christmas can bring such mixed feelings, especially for those who have suffered loss of health or jobs, making family relations strained. Too many children grow up in our time

Maggie Beth Phelps gets a snuggly new bear for Christmas.

dreading the holidays, with alcohol and violence taint-ing the days with uncertainty and sadness and painful memories.

I was blessed to grow up in a family that knew Jesus. For us, Christmas was a cherished and happy time. Though we were not wealthy, and the gifts were neither lavish nor extravagant, my parents always managed to have something nice under the tree for us five kids. My most treasured gift ever was a pair of white figure skates. Opening up that boxed gift was about the most magical of any of my childhood memories. ✳

Solveig Leithaug's daughter, Kari Henderson, is snuggled in and ready for some gift wrapping.

DEAN HOPPER
A New Bike

Let me give you a little background on my very earli-est Christmas memory. I was only three years old, and we had just built a new house on property that my mother's family had previously owned. My grandparents lived about a half-mile south of us, down in a valley. I adored playing there year 'round, but especially at Christmas.

We lived in the country, just off the main road on a gravel street. The path to my grandparents' house was in even worse condition, but that didn't hinder me from taking off down there as often as my little toddler legs could carry me. Grandpa had a small farm and I loved helping out; I credit my knowledge of tractors to that man, and I thought it was heaven.

Mom and Dad didn't mind me running off to Grandma and Grandpa's place, but it was a pretty long walk. I had a small bicycle with training wheels that didn't travel so well in the gravel. I needed new transportation, and it was (conveniently) Christmastime,

This old photograph shows the well-worn dirt path to Dean's grandparents' house, which his new bike would travel countless times after that special Christmas morning.

so I asked for a bicycle. Even at age three, I selected the particular kind and size. They called it the "Spider Bike": it had big wheels, huge handlebars, and a banana seat—which meant the seat was elongated and could be adjusted up or down in the back. The best part was its three gears. This bike could FLY down the road.

Now as I said before, I had been riding my little bike with the training wheels, and had made the best of it, but I couldn't contain the excitement I had built up for the new one I was hoping to find under the tree on Christmas morning. When I awoke and sprang to the living room, I was ecstatic to see my new bike sitting there, topped with one of my mother's famous big bows. Immediatcly I noticed that it didn't have training wheels. Nerve wracking. I had ridden my neighbor's bike without training wheels once or twice, but nothing to prepare me for this "mac daddy." To say the least, my anxiety was very high. Mom helped steady me as I got on . . . while in the house. I asked if I could ride right out the front door, and surprisingly, she said yes. I did, and was doing great until I got to the middle of the front yard, where I crashed to my unexpected doom. Just kidding.

It only hurt a little, but it taught me a lot. I got back on the bike and rode all over the yard, up the road, and eventually down to my grandparents' house. It became my mode of transportation for several years to come. It was a great Christmas to remember. ❄

TANYA GOODMAN-SYKES
The Hottest New Doll

For my daughter Mallory's second Christmas, she had been wanting a doll. Every time she'd see one, she'd say, "Dolly, wanna dolly." Michael and I had already bought her Christmas gifts—the main one being one of those toddler-sized play kitchens by Little Tikes with a sink, a fridge, and an oven. But Mallory had been pretty insistent about a doll, so we went out and bought her a big old floppy baby doll that was almost as big as she was.

The first thing she did

Fortunately, baby Molly survived her toasty trip to the play oven and is pictured here getting a big hug from Mallory.

Christmas morning was pick up the baby, put it on her shoulder, and pat it, cooing, "Baby, baby . . ." Then she went right over to the Little Tikes kitchen, casually opened the oven door, put the baby doll inside, closed the door, and started opening her other presents. I'm pretty sure that if we'd had a video of that, we could have won the $100,000 prize from *America's Funniest Home Videos*. ❄

LYNDA RANDLE
Thank You, Baby Jesus

Christmas was always a very special time in our family, and it still is. We were very blessed as children to have a mom and dad who loved us very much and who loved each other dearly. We may not have had a lot of money, but we did have a lot of love.

I can remember one Christmas morning in particular. I was up at the crack—and I mean the crack—of dawn. I couldn't get downstairs to our tree fast enough, but it was with mixed emotion. You see, there was this one baby doll that I really wanted: Baby Alive. She was, at that time, my heart's only desire; all I wanted for Christmas.

When I told my parents about her a few weeks earlier, they told me our Christmas budget was really small; and because there were six children in our home, we might not be able to have certain things. This broke my little heart, but I certainly understood the financial position we were in at that time—or did I? I still hoped for a miracle somehow, that just maybe my parents could get enough money so I could have my special doll.

Well, over thirty years later, I am happy to report that when I got to the tree that morning, my sweet Baby Alive doll was nestled safely below. To this day, I still don't know how my parents made that happen; but they did, and I am grateful. What a beautiful Christmas morning it was.

There was another beautiful Christmas morning

*Liam Gaither making
a snow angel.*

that changed the entire course of history, and the Gift of that morning is still changing history and lives today. Unlike my doll that only brought me temporary pleasures, Jesus—the everlasting Prince of princes—was truly the best gift my parents ever gave to me, and I am eternally grateful.

So may this Christmas be the most beautiful and memorable morn ever, even if you don't get the gift you so desire. Just know that the best Gift of all is still waiting to be unwrapped. Receive Him today, my friend. ❊

Joy and her girls singing "Heirlooms" at their annual Christmas Eve candlelight service the night before Joy got the big news!

JOY GARDNER
A Real Baby!

For most of my girls' lives, we participated in a Christmas Eve candlelight service where Dionne, Lauren, and I would sing a medley of the songs "Heirlooms" and "I Love to Tell the Story" as a trio. Continuing our tradition during Christmas 2002, we were singing together, and I noticed that Lauren cried through the medley.

It wasn't until the next morning—when Landy and I opened our gifts from Dionne and her husband, Scott—that I realized why: a big pink cup for me and a big blue cup for Landy, each containing an ultrasound picture.

Dionne had shared her news with her sister earlier, so as not to steal the thunder of Lauren's Christmas morning; and I suddenly understood that those tears had been tears of joy! We were going to be grandparents! Christmastime has always been a time of unexpected announcements and surprising adventures in my life. Not only was I born in December, but the news of both my daughters' births and my grandson's birth came during this blessed season. ❊

GORDON MOTE
Feeling the Gifts

When I was a kid, I could figure out what was inside the Christmas packages better than anyone. I would never open any present, and my parents knew I wouldn't, but I could still figure out what was inside if I could just get my hands on it and rattle it. My

The Mote family Christmas tree, all loaded with gifts and ready for Christmas morning.

The Motes (with their Norwegian friend, Pauline [far left], who spent her senior year with them) are all ready to dig into their Christmas morning gifts.

JOY GARDNER
Gift Wrapping with Gusto

Wrapping gifts at our house is a family event. We light a fire in the fireplace; gather paper, ribbons, tape, and scissors; and settle in for an all-night affair. We turn on *It's a Wonderful Life* or *The Christmas Story*, and I make hot chocolate and popcorn. We take pride in each package being carefully decorated, and when we are finished, the splendor of the wrapping almost outweighs the contents of the package!

The importance of the presentation of our gifts was passed down to us from Landy's father, who would spend hours a day for months before Christmas, hot-gluing beautifully crafted bows, handmade ornaments, and fresh flowers on each gift. One year, the boxes were so extravagant that he rented a U-Haul to

wife, on the other hand, would always search the closets and hunt down her gifts. With most kids, if the gifts are out of sight when they check the closet, the gifts are safe. But she would tear the closet apart, and if there were presents in there, she would find them!

After Kimberly and I got married, I told her she didn't have to wrap mine. But she wanted me to have the experience of unwrapping them just like she did. And she was right. Unwrapping gifts is great, and I always appreciate the time she took to choose something she knew I would love and wrap it for me.

Choosing gifts for Kimberly and the kids is one of my favorite parts of Christmas. You don't have to have eyes to make a personal choice. If you know your family well, you know what they would like, or want, or need, or would never buy for themselves. So finding that special gift is a lot of fun, and it shows the people in our lives that we know and love them.

I want to show my family I love them all year long, and Christmas is a great time to communicate that love through giving. ❅

drive them to Nashville from West Virginia—not because there were so many gifts, but because he wanted to lay each one out flat so his creations wouldn't touch each other and be crushed. We saved every one of those bows, and we recycle them every year, preserving the memory of the talent and care that my father-in-law took to make each gift special. ❅

Joy's father-in-law's creations still top their family's gifts year after year.

TANYA GOODMAN-SYKES
The "Unwrapping" Mystery

This is a story that's often told about me. I'm pretty sure my family is making it up, because I was a saintly child.

The story goes that very early one Christmas morning, when I was about three years old, my parents heard quite a racket coming from the living room. When my dad came in to investigate, every Christmas package under our tree had been ripped open, yet I was sitting calmly in a recliner, "reading" a book—which happened to be upside-down.

When Dad walked in, I never flinched or peered up from the book. He said "Tanya!" in a stern voice, and I jumped and shrieked. He asked why I jumped, to which I replied, "You just make me so nervous!"

I think my parents were so amused by my attempted cover-up that they didn't even scold me. Hey, I saved everybody a lot of trouble that year: their gifts were pre-opened! ❋

Calvin and Joyce Newton look on as their granddaughter, Samantha, opens her gift.

FEELING THE
Glory
~ *Calvin Miller* ~

This God is divinity,
begging you to reach and touch.
Touch what?
The human condition.
The rough texture
of a splintered wooden manger.
The night air on your skin.

❧

Then touch the celebration
that has reached your heart,
and widen yourself
to the whole of Christmas.
The rough bark of the evergreen that
speaks as Braille to your fingertips,
announcing that Jesus has
changed our despair to the kind of joy
that only angels know!

❧

Let the frost of the snow remind you
of the world's condition before He came,
and its shimmering brightness
of the cleansing covering that
leaves the most corrupt of us
pure in the eyes of God.

Continued on page 90

Touching a Hurting World *with* Christmas

And in our world of plenty
We can spread a smile of joy
Throw your arms around the world
At Christmastime.

BOB GELDOF AND MIDGE URE
"DO THEY KNOW IT'S CHRISTMAS?"

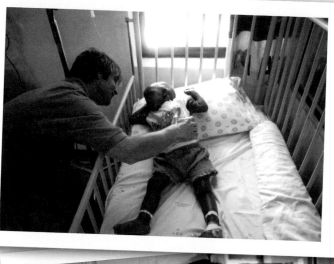

LADYE LOVE SMITH
Holding Christmas on the
Other Side of the World

One of our most special Christmas memories was the year Reggie and I spent time in South Africa with Samaritan's Purse at the children's hospital and school. We were there just before Christmas, and it was SO meaningful to us. We sang to the children, and they presented a play. Then we helped Samaritan's Purse hand out the Christmas shoeboxes, and it was an amazing experience. One of the orphans who was about ten years old came up to me and asked me to be her "new mother."

The kids were so excited, and they taught us a great deal about being grateful. All they got for Christmas was in that little shoebox, but they had so much more in their hearts!

Then we went to the hospital, where the children were terminally ill. We sang songs to them, and they opened their shoeboxes. Reggie and I visited some children who were too sick to come to the party. In the distance, I could hear a baby crying, and I went to her. She was all alone in a baby bed. I picked her up and

Many of the Homecoming artists participate in Angel Tree, Operation Christmas Child, and other wonderful giving projects at Christmas.

she stopped crying. There are so many children—most of them have no parents (due to AIDS), so the nurses cannot be with all of them all of the time. This baby clung to my neck, and I could hardly stand to put her down when it was time to leave. ❄

"The joy of brightening other lives,
bearing each others' burdens,
easing other's loads and supplanting
empty hearts and lives with generous gifts
becomes for us the magic of Christmas."

W. C. JONES

JASON CRABB
Angel Tree

Pictured here are Anthony Burger, Bill Gaither, and Lori Apple with Operation Christmas Child gifts donated by artists and fans.

Each Christmas we take part in an Angel Tree—where you take a name from the tree and read about the person's needs and then buy gifts for them, sort of like a Christmas wish.

One year we pulled three or four different names from the tree. They were little kids, and they needed some school clothes. So we bought the requested items in their sizes. But then there was a place on the card that explained what was going on with the particular family you were helping. The mother was a single mother raising three or four kids, and she hadn't expected to be in this situation. She was doing the best she could, but she just couldn't provide Christmas for them. And so Shelly and I went out, and we talked to a store and told them what we were doing, and they gave us great deals on some things.

One of the things on the kids' wish list was bicycles. We loaded up the truck with bikes and other stuff for the kids, and we got the mother something too. Well, when we pulled up in the yard that night and the kids came

out to the truck and we started handing them gifts, we said everything was from their mom—because, you know, they *were* from her. She went out on a limb to tell what needs her family had, and if she hadn't done that, those kids wouldn't have received anything.

Then we handed the mother the gift we'd bought for her, and she just cried and hugged us and said she couldn't believe that we would buy not only for her kids but for her. That's when it really hit home. Yes, we care for kids, and that's a no-brainer—we'll do for them. But what shocked me the most was how much it meant to her that we gave her something as well. When we left, the kids were having a blast, but the mother touched our hearts as much as the kids did.

So we learned a lesson that year: we really need to show love no matter what the age, no matter who it is. It was a good moment. One of those nice, warm-and-fuzzy moments where you think, *Wow, we didn't expect for that to happen, but how great that it did!* ❄

> WE REALLY NEED TO SHOW LOVE NO MATTER WHAT THE AGE, NO MATTER WHO IT IS.

Christmas, my child, is love in action.
DALE EVANS

KIM HOPPER
Paying It Back

When I was eight years old, my mom and dad felt so blessed that they decided to pay it back. A little over a week before Christmas, we loaded up the car and headed to Grandfather Mountain Children's Home. Four little beaming eyes approached our car as Emily and Amy, twin five-year-old girls from a broken home, saw they would be spending the holidays with a complete family this year. It's funny how refreshing sincerity in a child's eyes can be to even another child. To watch them excitedly approach our modest tree with the homemade ornaments and multicolored twinkling lights and accept the love and warmth our family offered them, is a memory I hope to never forget.

Christmas morning came, and Em and Amy were presented with their gifts. You would have thought Santa himself was in his sleigh in our living room, personally handing out presents while surrounded by reindeer and a small gaggle of elves! I was overwhelmed with gratitude and pride to realize that MY family brought their smiles! I imagine they had never experienced a holiday quite like this one. How surprising it was that such a typical Christmas for me was an extraordinary event for these girls.

I pray that Emily and Amy look back on those ten days as gratefully as I do. Though our objective was to bless someone else, I somehow think we were the ones being blessed. ❄

Holding Loved Ones Close

*Oh, I'm glad we'll be together
on this evening in December.
We'll watch the falling snow
and hold each other close.*

TRICIA WALKER
"AN EVENING IN DECEMBER"

SONYA ISAACS-YEARY
Love . . . an Unforgettable Ride

Romance and Christmas just go hand in hand . . . especially in Manhattan! Last year, my husband and I went to the city for a few days' visit. Jimmy is the only person I know who loves Christmas as much as I do, and this was his first time there. He was completely blown away! My very favorite memory of that trip (. . . and of my entire life) was taking a horse and buggy

ride through Central Park. I'll never forget how full my heart felt sitting next to my soulmate, cuddled up under a warm blanket, sipping hot chocolate in the cold, bustling air, watching all the shoppers hustle in and out of the stores as we rested our tired bodies in the comfort of the carriage. Christmas melodies filled the air, and snow trickled down gently, creating just the right dusting for the horses' hooves to leave their prints. It was a beautiful memory—one that I hope to relive many, many times!

Then, on December 20, 2009, I married my best friend. Jimmy and I had only met six months before, but we knew from our first date that it was meant to be. There, in the elegant ballroom of the historic Hermitage Hotel in Nashville, Tennessee, we said our vows surrounded by Christmas trees, wreaths, poinsettias, and a room full of dear friends who took time out of their busy holiday to celebrate our nuptials.

Sonya and Jimmy taking a carriage ride in NYC (above left); Sonya and Jimmy's Christmas wedding (above), December 20, 2009.

We even wrote a song together to sing at the wedding. The chorus says: "Feels like Christmas here with you, all my wishes coming true/Every day's a gift because you love me like you do/Feels like Christmas the whole year through." And that's exactly how it's felt ever since that wonderful day! ❆

CHARLOTTE RITCHIE
Christmas with Mom

In November of 1991, we were informed that my mom had two tumors in her abdomen that would require surgery. The doctor was certain it was cancer, and surgery was scheduled to take place a week before Christmas. We were upset but hopeful.

The day of the operation, they took Mom into surgery, and my dad anxiously sat in the waiting room. After what seemed like days, the doctor came to inform him the surgery had gone well—but more important, there was no cancer! We were so thankful!

That Christmas morning, Dad brought Mom out to the sofa, sat her down, and placed a big red bow around her neck. We all cried tears of joy and thankfulness because we had been given such a wonderful gift. ❆

LADYE LOVE SMITH
Christmas with Daddy

My eighty-seven-year-old daddy usually spends Christmas Eve and Christmas morning with us. He is here for our Christmas Eve service and dinner afterwards, which is always followed by us playing music until midnight! He is also here in the morning after Santa comes, and we have a big breakfast like my mother always did. Then we open the presents by the tree! ❆

FEELING THE
Glory
~ *Calvin Miller* ~

Reach for the lights of Christmas
as they illuminate
our streets and houses.
Touch the cold stone of a cathedral,
and remember that the chill of death
has been replaced
by the warmth of reconciliation.
Then, offer a warm hand
to those who need the
thawing grace of Christ's forgiveness.

It is Christmas.
Gently reach out and touch the hostel
and the hospital dwellers.
Let the Baby who took on flesh,
use your flesh
To offer up the
most touching truth of Christmas:
God is with us.
We are not alone.

DEAN HOPPER
Uncle Charles

Our family always spent Christmas Eve with my mother's relatives. My mom's brother, Uncle Charles Henry Shelton—first of seven children—was born in 1922. None of us are exactly sure what happened during birth, but he lived a physically and mentally challenged life. He struggled to understand the simplest of things. His coordination was affected, and he needed assistance with tasks like bathing. But he was strong, and he worked hard to do his part on the farm. I saw him lift and carry one-hundred pound feed bags in either arm when it was time for field work.

Uncle Charles was simply a joy to be around. His favorite Christmas song, "Up on the Housetop," was a staple during the holiday season. Mom would play the tune on the piano while we all sang, and Charles was the loudest, of course. He lived with my grandparents until they passed away, then with his older brother until he passed.

Yes, he definitely outlived all of the doctors' speculations. By that time, Charles was

Dean enjoys every moment with his favorite uncle. This was one of Uncle Charles's last Christmases.

in his late seventies and decided to reside in a small country rest home near my parents' house. No matter where he lived through the years, we always had our time with Uncle Charles. He was simply the greatest Christmas guest ever!

He had a love and concern for his family that was unusually strong. He loved his neighbors and friends like family. He enjoyed getting to know folks he had never met before, even those he would never see again. He would often ask about a particular person he had met some twenty years earlier, and would still remember their conversation—where they were from, what they liked to eat, and even their habits. He was amazing.

Although Uncle Charles had trouble with many of life's mundane tasks, he had some very special gifts. He couldn't read a watch or clock, but he could tell you the exact time of day, and was never off by more than five minutes. Mom once told me that she would only get down out of her father's lap to get up in Charles's lap; he would rock her to sleep. Come to think of it, he used to rock me too. ❅

JEFF & SHERI EASTER
Crowding In

In 2010, two weeks before Christmas, our oldest child, Madison, married his high school sweetheart of six

Madison and Shannon Easter's beautiful December wedding made for an extra-special (and extra-crowded) Christmas at Jeff and Sheri Easter's home!

years. The wedding was beautiful. They chose to be married in an historic cultural center decorated in beautiful Christmas colors. Jeff's family lives several hours away, and they rarely get to visit. But because the wedding was so close to Christmas, they all came in for the weekend to celebrate. At one time we counted forty-plus relatives staying in and around our house, filling bedrooms, bus bunks, next-door rental houses, and our guesthouse. Family was everywhere, and it was thrilling. ❅

The Chill ...and the Warmth

JIM MURRAY
Wet Socks and Hot Chocolate

Isn't it amazing how so many memories of our childhood are locked up in our senses? It only takes a whiff of something baking in the oven to unlock them.

I have lived in Nashville for more than forty-five years, but I grew up in Michigan, where the winter always provided enough snow to make snow angels, play ice hockey, and ride our sleds. The crunch of wet snow reminds me of the times we would take our sleds down the street, cross over busy Saginaw Avenue and then over Michigan

Avenue, cross a fence (that I now know is a golf course), and head up the steep slopes to where the "whees" were!

Every now and then our "whees" were interrupted by a mean ol' man who would chase us off the property. We'd drag our sleds and ourselves, our clothing wet and heavy, back to the house where Mom would fix hot chocolate and we could relax and recount our frigid adventures.

Ahh, the smell of hot chocolate and wet socks . . . those were the days. ❋

"Like snowflakes, my Christmas memories gather and dance—each beautiful, unique and too soon gone."

DEBORAH WHIPP

JOY GARDNER
The Feel of Snow

It usually doesn't snow in Nashville, but we recently got a beautiful snow on Christmas! Snow is so pure . . . the texture of it and the purity of it makes you feel something that is hard to describe. Getting out in it and enjoying its freshness brings a sense of newness. Somehow, when you feel it fall on your skin, it puts you in contact with nature and you are able to enjoy the beauty of the season in a way that nothing else quite captures.

IVAN PARKER
A Snowy Surprise

I remember so well when I was just a small boy growing up in a rural town in North Carolina. As most young boys do on Christmas Eve once they've been tucked into bed, I was thinking of everything I had asked for that I wanted for Christmas and was wondering if I'd left anything out. One of the most important items was snow! I wanted so badly to wake up on Christmas morning to a snowy surprise.

I happen to be the youngest of seven children, so naturally I had to go to bed first. When the last brother came up to bed that night, he did as he often did before climbing between the covers: he opened the window in his bedroom. However, on this night he forgot to close it before he fell asleep, and we all woke up the next morning to screaming instead of Christmas cheer! We ran to check the commotion . . . snow had covered his entire bed and the floor! We laughed as we all cleaned up the snow. It didn't bother me at all: I had my Christmas morning wish! ❋

Oh the weather outside is frightful,
But the fire is so delightful . . .

SAMMY CAHN AND JULE STYNE
"LET IT SNOW"

DAVID & LORI PHELPS
The Lazy Sledders

One of our favorite family pastimes is playing in the snow. We don't get much snow in Tennessee—maybe one good snow every two or three years—so it's always exciting to get out in it. And for us, playing in the snow is not just for the kids, it's a family affair. We have snowball fights and sled down the hills on our farm. And we have figured out a system that makes it even more fun.

After we sled down the hill, David takes us back up the hill on the four-wheeler, so we never have to trudge up the hill lugging our sleds behind us! I guess you could call us the lazy sledders! ❄

KARINA RHODE
A Warm Ukranian Blessing in the Freezing Cold

Seems like I remember it being 2 or 3 a.m. As a bleary-eyed six-year-old, I was being rousted out of bed by my father. There was no emergency to answer to. By all rights and privileges of childhood, I had every excuse to bury myself under the covers and ignore the wake-up call (at least once). Instead, like Rocky Balboa in the final round of a fight, I fought the urge to revisit an unconscious state. This would be no run-of-the-mill 3 a.m.

Dad and Mom helped my sister and me into our winter attire, though I was still in my pajamas. I don't think I even had socks on, but I was too excited to notice how cold my feet were inside my boots. My hands were busy playing with the pocket full of dry, uncooked rice Dad had given me. Pitch black and "brisk," as my father called it, was that morning. Snow was on the ground, but the walk had been shoveled, revealing a clear path to Grandma's house. Sneaking quietly up to Grandma's front door, Dad hushed our excited giggles. Ironic, considering how he shattered that brief moment of silence an instant later as he beat on Grandma's front door with the ferocity of a bass drummer in a parade.

A flutter of what sounded like two squirrels falling out of a tree came from inside the house. Lights ignited indoors, quickly followed by a flood of porch lights. Someone inside frantically fumbled with the deadbolt, and the door flew open, revealing my grandmother. A mass of disheveled silver hair hanging down to her waist and in her nightgown—this was not the woman I was used to seeing in a dress, apron, and neatly pinned braid about her head.

Despite our shock at seeing Grandma in this condition, my sister and I sprung into action. Proceeding to pelt Grandma's shins and living room carpet with rice, we shouted, *"Seeu Seeu Posevau Znovym Rokom Pozdravlau!"* Grandpa was yelling something I didn't understand while Grandma shrieked, grabbed her purse, and proceeded to empty the contents of her wallet into our rice-riddled hands.

In this day and age, one might interpret this scene to be more than a bit alarming. But one look at the delight on my grandmother's face, and you'd know different. What we had just uttered was a most treasured Ukrainian New Year's blessing. This was the first time my sister and I had taken part in this cherished family tradition—and it wouldn't be the last.

The verse we spoke that morning translates roughly to "Sowing, sowing, sowing, and wishing you a prosperous new year!" I still remember sitting at the kitchen table memorizing a phonetic version of the verse Dad had scrawled on a piece of notebook paper: *See-you see-you paw-see-viy-you snaw-vim rock-em paws-drawv-lieyem.*

As Dad tells the story of this Ukrainian tradition: "Before the second World War, 90 percent or more of the people lived on and made their living from small truck farms. We raised our own food in the garden and in the fields, and we had all kinds of animals: cows,

pigs, chickens, ducks, geese, turkeys, rabbits, etc. So we depended heavily on good crop years to feed ourselves and the animals.

"In Ukraine, it was tradition on New Year's Day to go house to house, waking people up, reciting this verse of blessing, and throwing grain into the home. You had to go early to catch the farmers before they left for the fields. It was believed that performing this simple act would bless the household and crop for the entire year to come.

"Ukrainians were very superstitious, so they put a lot of value in getting many New Year's wishes. In the unfortunate event a household was missed, there would be much anxiety that the year's harvest would be poor. For those households who did receive the blessing, the blessed house would reward the well-wishers with money, food, or drink as thanks for the blessing received."

So there it was. A mess of dry rice on my grandmother's carpet that she would refuse to vacuum up for over a week. We'd received our reward—pockets stuffed full of money—but our work wasn't done yet. Fortunately for us, there were three more unsuspecting Ukrainian families in the neighborhood, and the morning was still young—as were we.

Thirty-two years later, my family still carries on this tradition. It's done over the phone now, and the earliest we call is 6 a.m. (But that's another story. Let's just say that neither of our husbands is Ukrainian, and leave it at that.) Even if we miss New Year's Day, we'll manage to call the day after. And no matter how or when it's delivered, the sentiment is still the same: we take the time to bless each other's new year with these most treasured words in our family tradition.

I couldn't explain it then, but those years we failed to call on-time felt like something was missing until I heard

> SO THERE IT WAS. A MESS OF DRY RICE ON MY GRANDMOTHER'S CARPET THAT SHE WOULD REFUSE TO VACUUM UP FOR OVER A WEEK.

that Ukrainian verse. Today, I believe the emptiness I felt then is connected to an inherent desire for our Father's blessing of prosperity in our lives.

My earthly father's family tradition is a gentle reminder to me that my heavenly Father desires His children to be blessed, and to prosper, and to share that blessing with each other. Without that exchange, we would indeed feel an intense void.

Tradition can be a powerful tool to share a spiritual truth with the younger generation. Although I have no children of my own, I have three nephews who I pray will carry on this tradition of blessing for years to come—a gentle reminder to them that the blessing of prosperity is theirs to give and to receive.

Maybe I'm just a sucker for tradition, but I still anticipate the day my sister might bring her boys to my front door at 3:00 in the morning to make a "blessed" mess in the name of family tradition that I'll be in no hurry to clean up.

I am honored to share this tradition with you, and to say to your household:

"Seeu Seeu Posevau Znovym Rokom Pozdravlau!" ❅

DAVID & LORI PHELPS
One Unforgettable Fire

Our home was built in 1815 and has two stone fireplaces. When we moved to our Tennessee farm, we were excited about cutting our own firewood from trees on our own property to start a warm, cozy fire when the temperatures dropped.

It didn't take us long to discover, though, that cutting our own firewood is no light work! It comes with lots of sore muscles, calluses, and tired arms. Still, we felt such a sense of accomplishment when it came time to light our first fire of the season. We gathered our logs, and before long, we could feel that wonderful fire permeate the room. But as the logs grew brighter and the fire grew hotter, we both began sneezing and sneezing . . . and sneezing. And sneezing! It didn't take long for us to realize that there were cedar logs mixed in with our hardwood. (We are both extremely allergic to cedar!)

We still love to light cozy fires in the fireplace, but we now know to make sure there is no cedar among the firewood! ❅

KEVIN WILLIAMS
Overheated Santa

A few years ago, the folks at our church decided to include Santa Claus in the Christmas program. Even though he clearly had no part in the biblical Christmas story, he was there to read "The Night Before Christmas" and pass out candy to the kids. What Santa didn't count on was the extra-heavy costume and beard, the dry winter air, and the fourteen steps leading up to the stage. It's possible, too, that he hadn't considered his extra weight to be a liability, until he tackled the fourteen steps.

By the time he ran up on stage and greeted and gathered all the children around, Santa was too exhausted to read the story. He panted heavily as he struggled through, "Twas the night . . . before Christmas . . . and all . . . through the house . . ." By the time he was ready to "tear open the window and throw back the sash," Santa was out of air, huffing and puffing like the big, bad wolf. His face was as red as his suit, and sweat was dripping from underneath his beard.

The crowning moment came when he stopped the story, closed the book, and said, "Whew! Can somebody get Santa some water? It's hot as July up here!" ❄

Heap on the wood!
The wind is chill;
But let it whistle as it will,
We'll keep our Christmas merry still.

SIR WALTER SCOTT

Coby Phelps gets in his Christmas wish, and it looks like Santa is holding up better than he did at Kevin's church!

Embracing Change

GLORIA GAITHER
My Most Memorable Christmas

I f everything special and warm and happy in my formative years could have been consolidated into one word, that word would have been *Christmas*. So, by the time the building blocks of my days had piled themselves into something as formidable as late adolescence, Christmas had a lot to live up to.

By then, Christmas meant fireplaces and the bustle of a big, excited family complete with aunts, uncles, and cousins. It meant great smells from the kitchen—homemade bread, and cranberries bubbling on the stove, pumpkin pies, and turkey. It meant Grandma's cheery voice racing to be the first to holler, "Christmas gifts!" as we came through the door. It meant real cedar Christmas trees, handmade foil ornaments, and lots of secrets. It meant enfolding in the arms of our great family the lonely or forsaken of our village who had no

place to go. It meant all the good and lovely things we said about Christmas being in the heart and the joy being in the giving.

Then came that one year.

There were many things that conspired, as it were, to bring me to the laboratory situation in which I would test all my so-glibly-accepted theories. Grandma was gone, leaving in my heart a vacuum that wouldn't go away. My sister was married now, and had the responsibility of sharing her holidays with her husband's family. The other relatives were far away. After a lifetime of serving in the ministry, Daddy felt directed that year to resign the pastorate of his flock with no other pastures in mind and "wait on the Lord." Since I was away at college, just beginning my first year, I wasn't there when my parents moved from the parsonage to the tiny cottage at the lake that a concerned businessman had helped them build. Nor was I prepared that winter day for the deserted barrenness that can be found in resort areas built only for summertime fun.

There was no fireplace. There was no bustle of a big, excited family. Gone was the sense of tradition and history that is the art of the aged to provide, and gone was the thrill of the immediate future that comes with the breathless anticipation of children.

The dinner was going to be small—for just the three of us—and there wasn't any ring in the brave attempt at shouting "Christmas gifts!" that Mother made as I came in the door. Daddy suggested that because I'd always loved it, he and I should go to the woods to cut our own tree. I knew that now, of all times, I could not

AS I PICKED UP MY END OF THE SCRAGGLY, DISAPPOINTINGLY SMALL CEDAR, I ALSO PICKED UP MY END OF GROWN-UP RESPONSIBILITY.

let my disappointment show. I put on my boots and my cheeriest face, and off through the knee-deep snow we trudged, into the Michigan woods. My heart was heavy, and I knew Mother was back at the stove, fighting back the tears for all that was not there.

There was a loveliness as the forest lay blanketed in its heavy comforter of snow, but there was no comforter to wrap around the chill in my heart. Daddy whistled as he chopped the small cedar tree. (He always whistled when there was something bothering him.) As the simple, tuneless melody cut through the silent, frozen air, I got a hint of the silent burdens adults carry, and for the first time felt myself on the brink of becoming one. So as I picked up my end of the scraggly, disappointingly small cedar, I also picked up my end of grown-up responsibility. I felt the times shift. I was no longer a child to be sheltered and cared for and entertained. My folks had put good stuff in me. Now, as I trudged back through the snow, watching the back of my father's head, the weary curve of his shoulders, his breath making "smoke signals" in the morning air, I vowed to put some good stuff back into their lives.

The day was somehow different after that. We sat around our little tree stringing cranberries and making foil cut-outs. But this time, it was not the activity of a child, but a sort of ceremonial tribute to the child I somehow could never again afford to be, and to the people who had filled that childhood with such wealth and beauty. ❄

EXCERPTED FROM *LET'S MAKE A MEMORY: CREATING FAMILY TRADITIONS* BY GLORIA GAITHER AND SHIRLEY DOBSON

KIM HOPPER
Christmas at the Ocean

Growing up in the mountains of North Carolina, it wasn't unusual to have several inches of snow on the ground by Christmas. Our typical Christmas was spent wrapped up in a warm blanket by the fire and surrounded by our loved ones. However, one particular year it was completely different.

Because of some major health issues, my brother, Tim, was medically forced to move to the coast of North Carolina for the purifying oceanic air. His allergies were so severe that he could only go to certain newer restaurants or stores, and he could hardly be around any of his own family in a small, enclosed space. So that year, our many immediate families loaded up and headed to the beach for a coastal Christmas. The gifts were exchanged under a picnic shelter at the end of a pier, and instead of sitting in a warm home watching a game, we bundled up and played beach volleyball in forty-degree weather. We were frozen—but had a blast!

This may have not have been a traditional Christmas for us, but it reminded us of simple truths: no matter the circumstances, when surrounded by friends and family, you can celebrate anything . . . anywhere. ❄

SOLVEIG LEITHAUG
Blending Families

My husband, Jim, and I were married in 2009, and for Christmas that year we decided to drive nineteen-plus hours (one way) with David, Kari, and John from Nashville, Tennessee, to Boston, Massachusetts, in order to spend time with my stepsons, Elliott and Taylor, who were unable to get time off from their work and studies to travel home. We stayed in Taylor's bachelor apartment, played games, cooked, baked, and ate some fabulous food (my husband is a hobby gourmet chef, and the kids are following quickly in his steps). We saw a bit of Boston and made some great memories.

The photo shows a scrumptious fruit tart that Taylor and Kari made together. Our only decoration was a

Together Solveig's daughter, Kari, and Jim's son, Taylor, created a beautiful fruit tart for their newly blended family's first Christmas together.

two-and-half-foot fake Christmas tree we had brought from home. Although it will be awhile until we drive this stretch again, it was absolutely worth the many hours in the car to have a chance to be together, all seven of us. ❄

WOODY WRIGHT
Snowed In

My most interesting Christmas was 1980 or so, when I spent the holiday at my mother's house after a rare snow and ice storm hit our small, East Tennessee hometown. No one could get a vehicle up the large hill that leads to our place, so it was just my mother and me.

We normally have a big family breakfast on Christmas morning, with the centerpiece being our beloved chocolate syrup and homemade biscuits. Since the power was out, I started a fire in the fireplace to warm things up. Then Mother got creative and prepared our family favorite for the two of us in a skillet over the fire! What an adventure! ❄

AMY GAITHER-HAYES
It's Still Christmas

We're learning that even though traditions are important to us, the fact of the matter is, life changes. And people change. People die, and the house that we used to do things in isn't there anymore; and the people who used to cook are gone now, or can't cook anymore; and some of us have moved away, and we're starting our own traditions with our own families.

So maybe we can't all be together on Christmas morning like when we were little. Things do change, and guess what? The world doesn't fall apart. And not only that—it turns out that Christmas is very portable! You can take it with you wherever you are. It doesn't have to

be "the way it's always been" to be wonderful.

Thankfully, I don't feel panicked anymore about the thought of everything changing. God has given me such a peace about it all. The important things are still intact. Our connections to one another haven't lessened; in fact, they've strengthened. So wherever Christmas is this year, and whatever it looks like, I know it will be all right. The traditions will still be alive whether we get to practice them all together or not. And it's still Christmas. (Although I'm really going to be bummed if I don't get to have mom's chipped beef and gravy with homemade biscuits—I've been craving that all year!) ❄

Feeling *our* Humanity

Lord, my body is throbbing from fatigue from all the Christmas preparations.
When I stop to consider the Messiah and His coming, I can't stop my mind.
I keep making mental lists of details—
names I want to remember, things I have yet to do, and foods I must buy or prepare.
But I'm not complaining, Lord.
I love having a reason to do special things in Your name for people I love.
I am grateful that Your coming makes the whole world sing!
The business of Christmas breaks us all—even those who don't know You for themselves—
from the craze of commerce for profit and accomplishment and turns our attention to others.

The bell-ringers of the Salvation Army have become as much a part of the joy as Santa at the mall.
And although the crèche can no longer be assembled in the city square,
more of us are taking time to tell the children in our families
why we make the manger and its tiny occupant such a part of our homes.
More than ever as a new century is emerging,
I feel the urgency to make for another generation a celebration
that will make this the most important event of the year.
This must not become just another day or even just another holiday.
We must tell each other and the children that this babe in a manger
was and is the coming together of heaven and earth.

But, Lord, help me keep that focus in my own heart.
Help me remember that there is nothing of value that doesn't demand sacrifice and effort.
You, Yourself came on a quiet night in a small town,
but it wasn't the idyllic, effortless night depicted in the windows.
There was blood and water and pain.
There were insufficient provisions and fear.
There were visitors at a time when Mary must have wanted privacy.
From then on, You were putting Your own needs
as a human being on the back burner for the Big Picture.

So, it is not out of character for Christmas to be
wonderful and demanding, a time when fatigue and effort
are invested for a few amazing moments of glory.
It is for love.
All this day, let me remember—it is for love.

EXCERPTED FROM *A BOOK OF SIMPLE PRAYERS*
BY GLORIA GAITHER
(Ventura, CA: Regal/Gospel Light, 2008)

LILY ISAACS
Itching and ER Visits

In 1976, Ben got the chicken pox just a few days before Christmas. We had just decorated our little house, and put up a small tree, and made ornaments out of tin foil, macaroni, and construction paper. Then we'd added a string of small Christmas lights. We were proud of this little tree. We called it our "Charlie Brown Christmas tree." I knew it would make little Ben feel better too.

His fever was getting high, so Joe and I decided he needed to go to the doctor again. I took Ben and left Sonya (age three) and Becky (age two) at home with Joe. While at the doctor's office, I got a call from Joe. He said to hurry home because Becky had chewed up and swallowed a Christmas light bulb! I drove home in a panic.

As soon as Ben and I got there, Joe and I loaded up all the kids and headed to the Wilmington Hospital emergency room. After sitting there for several hours, the doctor x-rayed Becky's digestive tract and said he was sure that the rest of the plastic bulb would pass through. We screened everything she ate, and yes, soon enough, there it was! We were grateful she was okay!

Ben got over the chicken pox, but within two weeks both Sonya and Becky had it too. Needless to say, our entire Christmas holiday was spent indoors, but we had a great time enjoying each other and being thankful for what we did have. ❅

Lori and Luann Burger pause to enjoy the Christmas tree and refocus their attention on the Reason for this glorious season.

LORI APPLE
Fighting the Distractions

Christmas has become all about poinsettias that die, gifts that are forgotten in a week, and gluttony that often forgets how this day came about. So much of our mental space is spent on who is sitting where and who gets what—and that is just during the pastor's sermon! Yes, we have a lot of responsibilities, along with company coming or holiday travel. But don't let the meaningful become the meaningless.

I love the build-up leading to Christmas. I admit that I try to make my holiday decorations look as if a magazine photographer will arrive any minute. Still, that isn't the reason for celebrating. It's the why. Why is my family able to gather? Why does God give us so much when we give so little to Him? Why do we often forget that He came for us?

Growing up in a family who cherished the true meaning of Christmas has made it easy to continue that tradition in my adult life. It's easy to get lost in the commercialization of it all. But, what's the point of celebrating when you don't know why? Take time to remember the why this Christmas. ❅

GUY PENROD
Wrestling with Chaos

With Christmas always comes a little bit of chaos—what Angie calls "happy chaos." But having a house full of eight active kids, we have to work really hard to create moments and fight the noise and pandemonium that could easily take over.

The days leading up to Christmas are crazy, and we always have a family baking night, which is fun and a little messy. But on Christmas Eve, we gather the kids together and read the Christmas story from Luke 2. We wake up Christmas morning and have coffee and cinnamon rolls, and we take turns opening gifts one at a time. I'm not kidding when I say that sometimes it takes us two days to get through the gifts! Even so, there are often missing pieces or parts of something before it's over.

Then, every year after the last gift has been opened, Angie and I will look at each other and ask, "Did we do a little better this year at helping our kids understand this holy holiday?" We miss the mark plenty, and we always find ourselves a little disappointed that Christmas didn't go exactly as we wanted. We hope we did a few things right, and for all the ways we didn't, we ask for God's grace and learn something that we will apply the next year.

The very sense of inadequacy we feel—needing Him to show up in the midst of our chaos—is exactly why Jesus came in the first place. And this is just one of the million reasons we need His presence in our lives, not just at Christmas but every single day. We are human beings with broken, busy lives, trying to somehow internalize this event in history that we can barely wrap our brains around. Why He would want to leave heaven to dwell with a bunch of crazy yahoos like me, I'll never understand. But He did! And I'm so grateful.

Feeling Jesus' presence while corralling eight excited kids at Christmas isn't easy. But it's possible. We keep reminding ourselves, "All things are possible with Him"! ❋

> THE VERY SENSE OF INADEQUACY WE FEEL—NEEDING HIM TO SHOW UP IN THE MIDST OF OUR CHAOS—IS EXACTLY WHY JESUS CAME IN THE FIRST PLACE.

Touched *by the* Story

RUSS TAFF
Kissing Jesus

This is our favorite family Christmas card of all time. It was taken when Charlotte was about four years old. For some unknown reason in the middle of July, somebody had set up a complete manger scene across the street from us, in the front yard of the Reverend

Charlotte Taff gets it, even at four years old! Jesus wants us all to draw near to Him.

Becca Stevens. (We later figured out it was one of her practical-joking parishioners.) Little Charlotte was completely entranced with the whole thing, and we ended up with what is now a classic Taff family photo. ❋

> *When we recall Christmas past, we usually find that the simplest things—not the great occasions— give off the greatest glow of happiness.*
>
> BOB HOPE

LORI PHELPS
The Story Our Kids Will Remember

I used to be a teacher, which means I have a pretty large collection of children's Christmas books that I've gathered over the years. So I put stacks of kids' books about Christmas into big bas-

kets next to the fireplace in the living room and in the kitchen so that, if the opportunity presents itself at any point during the season, we can pull out a story and hopefully create a moment that the kids will remember.

I always hope that setting the atmosphere at home for Christmas will help our kids remember the specialness of this season and the importance of the Story. I'm constantly trying to grab those "June Cleaver, Leave It to Beaver" moments, and I always feel badly if I can't make them happen. But then I try to remember that many of my best childhood memories were small things that didn't seem like a big deal at the time.

My mom and my mother-in-law are often surprised by what David and I remember from when we were kids. In reality, the things that stuck with us were just simple little things that happened in passing. I take a lot of comfort in that, hoping that what I see as "creating moments" for my kids might be a lot sim-

For Unto Us A Child Is Born

pler than I've tried to make it. Maybe what they hear of the Story will not be as vivid in their memories as what they experienced. ❊

EMILY SUTHERLAND
(STAFF WRITER, GAITHER MUSIC COMPANY)
Wanting to Be Mary

I always wanted to be Mary in the Christmas pageant. Every year when it came time to cast the Christmas program, I would earnestly put on my holiest expression in hopes that the lady in charge would find me worthy of the star role. Mary always got to wear the prettiest costume rather than a drab bathrobe—or, worse, one of those white clone robes the angel choir had to wear! I wanted to be the main woman! The woman who was so special that God Himself chose her to parent His Son.

It took no talent, I thought, to slap on a white robe and a flimsy halo to squeak out a couple anemic versions of "Hark the Herald Angels Sing" and "Away in a Manger." But each year I took my place in the angel choir, hoping the following year would be my year.

I believed that being the preacher's kid might win me some advantage, but no. Our churches subscribed to the philosophy that offering the pastor's daughter a key role would be showing favoritism. So . . . into the angel choir I would go, offering all the while to be a shepherd. I mean, the headpiece and the thick robe, combined with my boyish frame, would surely help me pass for a shepherd! Anything but an angel clone!

"We need your voice in the angel choir," is how the director would justify it. Yet I knew my voice wasn't audible amid all the others. Compliant yet disheartened, I would join the choir and wait for another chance next year.

As the years wore on and graduation from elementary school was imminent, I knew time was running out. The role of Mary was always given to a young female,

"My niece, Avery, must have inherited my longing to be Mary. She dressed up as Mary for the reading of Luke 2 during last year's family Christmas Eve gathering. I'm pretty sure that is the same headpiece Mom used for my Mary costume years earlier," says Emily Sutherland.

never an adolescent! My biological clock was ticking!

By the time I was in high school, Christmas pageants were replaced by cantatas and caroling. I was fine with that, since I didn't want to be the only fourteen-year-old in the little kids' Christmas pageant. But then one year, when I was sixteen years old, the youth group at our church in Cedar Falls, Iowa, decided to create a live Nativity in the field beside the church. From Thursday through Sunday before Christmas that year, cars could drive by and witness a life-sized reenactment of the Christmas story. Members of the youth group were assigned to fill certain roles on certain nights and, at long last, I had my chance to play Mary for one glorious evening.

Carpenters in our church created an incredible life-sized stable. Local farmers donated the use of their animals. My mom was on the costume team and spent weeks sewing realistic-looking robes, tunics, headpieces, and belts until the tips of her fingers were raw from needle-pricks.

When the first night of the live Nativity arrived, the church was buzzing with teenagers in turbans and robes. Dressed in layer after layer underneath our costumes, we were graciously provided with butter cookies and hot cocoa in the hopes that starting out with full stomachs might make the next three hours in the bitter Iowa cold more bearable.

The plastic doll we would use for the baby Jesus was dutifully waiting on a nearby chair. Apparently someone had decided that using a real baby for the part of Jesus for this chilly project might be a bit cruel and unusual. Actually, it was probably borderline "cruel and unusual" for teenagers too, but I wasn't about to complain! I had waited a decade for this.

Soon it was time to file across the church parking lot and take our places in the Nativity scene. When we were all in place, the bright floodlights came on, and there we were . . . an active bunch of teenagers with bellies full of treats and more energy than we knew what to do with, participating in the most tangible form of the Christmas story we had ever experienced.

As I sat beside the manger, holding our plastic version of baby Jesus, I felt surprisingly unglamorous. I hadn't anticipated the lumpy layers hidden from the view of onlookers, or the static electricity under the shiny blue headdress, or the physically painful gusts of

> WHEN THE FIRST NIGHT OF THE LIVE NATIVITY ARRIVED, THE CHURCH WAS BUZZING WITH TEENAGERS IN TURBANS AND ROBES.

cold that bit every inch of exposed skin and blew straight through all the layers of clothing. With watery eyes and clenched teeth, as if clenching might help fight the cold, I did my best to keep the swaddling clothes from "unswaddling" in the straight-line wind.

By the time we all got our bearings, we realized that a long line of cars had formed along the road nearby. It was truly an Iowa, "if you build it, they will come" kind of experience. Our scene was set back from the road just enough that onlookers certainly couldn't see our teeth chattering or our lumpy layers. In

From the time we are kids, we learn to interact with the story in tangible ways. Here, Bret Smith is playing Joseph.

fact, my dad could have probably put on that shiny Mary headpiece and passed for the Virgin Mary.

I don't know how this live Nativity affected those passersby, but I know that feeling the physical discomfort of "being Mary" for that short span of time forever changed my glamorized image of the real Story. I no longer had a drive-by understanding of the biblical story. I had stepped into it. I had smelled the hay, heard the cattle lowing, and understood a little more about what really happened in that stable the night Christ was born. This briefly uncomfortable Christmas experience couldn't have held a candle to the discomfort Mary endured. She didn't get a hot chocolate-and-cookie snack before stepping into that stable. Instead, she got a long journey on a donkey during her final days of pregnancy. Give me windburn any day! And parenting the Savior of the world? Who could ever prepare for that?

I'm now more than forty years old. I have experienced childbirth. Twice. I have feared for my children's health and safety. I know that familiar struggle between the desire to nurture our children and the need to back away so they can grow into the people they were created to be. I understand firsthand how daunting it is to raise any child, but how much more daunting it would have been to raise a member of the Trinity! I haven't buried a child like she did, or waited three grueling days to witness His resurrection, but this much I do know: I no longer want to be Mary.

I know now that I could never fully realize the weight of Mary's calling—or my own—by clinging to that plastic Jesus. But because of my brief encounter with that plastic Jesus, I could better appreciate the real Jesus. In my desire to be at the heart of the Story, I learned a valuable thing. Mary wasn't the star of the Story at all. It was Jesus. And anything or anyone short of Immanuel simply could never give any of us the grace and strength we need to walk the journey He has laid out for us.

In my youthful arrogance, I had tried to make the Christmas story about me for all those years. And if we are totally honest, isn't it always a little tempting to make Christmas about us? We so long to FEEL the importance of the Christmas story! We want to be part of the miracle! And yet what we inevitably discover is that we are a part of the miracle.

We can touch Jesus in a thousand different ways when we let Him meet us in life's cold, uncomfortable, unsuspecting places. ❊

> *"Christmas is not as much about opening our presents as opening our hearts."*
>
> JANICE MAEDITERE

REBECCA ISAACS BOWMAN
A Clean Heart for Christmas

I have always loved Christmas. I remember as a child, the smell of the wood stove burning fresh logs. What a feeling in the air! So much joy and love! It's as if you could literally embrace it.

I remember my parents working so hard all year, struggling to have enough money to buy a few presents to put under the tree, wanting to find a way to make each Christmas special. Looking back now, I never really cared what was under the tree. All I cared about was the family who was coming in and the time we had together. Don't get me wrong—I was a normal kid who was so excited to open the gifts they did buy, but I was happy with anything.

I smile at thinking about our first Christmas tree. It was the most simple-looking fake silver pine tree. It had a revolving multicolor light to brighten up the aluminum-foil branches. I also cherish the times we gathered together on Christmas morning: Dad, Mom, Ben, Sonya, and myself. As a tradition, we would read the story of the birth of our Lord and Savior and then join hands for prayer. Not the quick, "Thank You, Lord" prayers, but prayers of thanksgiving. We were not in a hurry when we prayed, for we had so much to thank God for each year.

I will never forget one particular Christmas morning—it was 1980, and I was five years old: I asked Jesus to be my Savior. That's the best gift I could ever receive. Still today, we begin each Christmas morning by reading about the birth of Jesus, and then we have a family prayer time. After that we open gifts, eat, play music, sing, and play games. What fun, spending the day with people I love and cherish! ❊

KEVIN WILLIAMS
Our Family Nativity

In 2004, when our daughters Carolina and Olivia were ages five and three, we realized that we had read the Christmas story so many times that the girls knew it as well as they could possibly know anything at their ages. So Kathy and I decided to create a more hands-on experience that might give them a unique perspective on the story of Jesus' birth.

We created a makeshift manger by the fireplace. We dressed as shepherds with bathrobes, flip flops, and towels on our heads, and Carolina's "Baby Rhonda" played the part of Jesus. I was holding Olivia for our "journey" to the manger as we sang "Silent Night" and read the story from Luke 2.

Today, the girls are ages twelve and nine, and I'm not sure how vividly they remember the experience, but Kathy and I will never forget how we felt when we put ourselves in Mary and Joseph's shoes and looked at Baby Rhonda as if she were our child . . . then imagined giving up that child! We could never do that. But that's exactly what God did.

To this day, every time we read the Christmas story we are reminded of the sacrifice Jesus made for us and how His Father must have felt to see His only child suffer and die for us. I hope, as the years go on, that we never forget what we learned from our little family Christmas play that Christmas Eve. ❊

Coby Phelps

The *Fragrance* OF CHRISTMAS

✳ ✳ ✳

If all I could remember of Christmas were
just the smells of the season,
I would still be rich with memories.

Come share the fragrance of Christmas.

❋ The fragrance of the real cedar tree my grandfather cut in the Michigan woods and brought into the old farmhouse.

❋ The smells of cranberries simmering, Grandma's bread baking in the oven, popcorn popping to string for the tree, and spicy pumpkin pies cooling on the kitchen counter.

❋ The fragrance of clean sheets and blankets from the cedar closets pulled up around my neck as I was tucked into bed to wait for faraway Christmas morning.

❋ My daddy's Old Spice and mother's Max Factor powder as they held me on their laps to read the sweet story from Luke 2.

❋ The warming smell of hickory logs burning in the pot-bellied stove that heated the seldom-used "front room" through these special days of celebration.

Shut your eyes, take a deep breath, and inhale the aromas of home.

Gloria Gaither

OUR OWN
Frankincense
~ *Calvin Miller* ~

Mary was only a poor young mother

when Jesus came into her life.

Think of her:

holding her infant child

when the wise men arrived.

Her poverty was made rich by

the kings of the East.

They opened their gifts—

gold and frankincense and myrrh.

Two of these were gifts of aroma,

costly balms that flooded the room

with divine smells.

Continued on page 119

Smell *the* Pine

*The week had passed swiftly, like a dream, a dream fragrant
with the smell of pine boughs and Christmas trees . . .*

MARGARET MITCHELL
GONE WITH THE WIND

SHERI EASTER
Real Trees from Uncle Johnny

One of my favorite childhood Christmas memories is when my great-uncle Johnny, who was a timber cutter, would bring in our family's tree each year. This marked the official beginning of the holiday season in our home. I can remember the strong scent of pine filling the house as Daddy would mount the tree in its stand. After several directions from Mama—"a little to the left, a little to the right"—the tree would then be deemed "perfect" and ready for Mama to begin the decorating. We kids would offer to decorate, and after a few short minutes would lose interest and leave the decorating solely to Mama.

These many years later, Christmases are similar in my house

now, with everyone losing interest and leaving the decorations to me. But I don't really mind. What I do miss most is having a live tree and that smell of pine. For reasons of simplicity, we use an artificial tree, but sometimes I wish we'd go to the extra trouble just to allow our noses to celebrate once again! ✳

GORDON MOTE
One Real Tree

I remember the first time Kimberly and I ever went to a tree farm. The smell of pine was all around us, and we loved it so much that we decided for the first time ever to bring home a real, live Christmas tree. We got it home, and it gave the house that great pine smell, and it was awesome—until the needles started falling off and it started to dry out. We were then faced with the age-old question: Is it really worth it to go to all the trouble of a real tree? I thought maybe it was worth it, because I loved that smell. But I didn't have to clean it up either!

That was the first and only year we had a real tree. When you think about it, even the artificial tree has a smell of its own. When we bring our tree out of storage every year and pull it out of the box, the tree and the cardboard and the basement create their own smell. Nothing in the world is exactly like it.

I wonder if a lot of people miss the real thing. Either way—real tree or not—the tree's unique smell means the Christmas season has arrived. ✳

ANDY ANDREWS
Our Annual Fraser Fir

Thinking of Christmas always makes me think of the smell of a big ol' fresh Christmas tree. Putting up the tree was always a big family thing growing up, and it's a big thing for me and Polly and the boys now. We still get a live tree every year—a Fraser fir—because of the smell of a real tree. As pretty as plastic trees can be, the smell of plastic does not raise my holiday spirit! ✳

"My first copies of Treasure Island *and* Huckleberry Finn *still have some blue spruce needles scattered in the pages. They smell of Christmas still."*

CHARLTON HESTON

THE FRAGRANCE *of* HOME

LUANN BURGER
The Smell of Family Fun

The fragrant scents of Christmas can evoke the greatest memories from our past and permeate the new memories we create. The aroma of fresh-cut evergreen trees, wreaths, garlands, and swags bathe the space with essential oils and bring the great outdoors into our homes. The heavenly smell of baked goods abounding with cinnamon, ginger, and peppermint, along with the sweet perfume of mulled cider, establish a sense of being home for the holidays, no matter where we find ourselves geographically.

Each Christmas I gaze with wonder at the fragrant and beautiful things surrounding me, and I allow the spirit of the season to capture my heart and fill me with the anticipation of days to come. From the delicate glass-blown ornaments nestled among the pine and fir branches to the twinkle of lights in the crisp-clean air outside, each Yuletide offering saturates my senses. When all the aromas and scents combine with the melodious carols, the sounds of laughter, and the "Merry Christmas" salutations, how can I not be joyously consumed with holiday cheer?

As a young child, it didn't take long to associate the delightful smells of the season with the highly anticipated

arrival of distant relatives and the excitement of celebrating Baby Jesus' birth. One of my most cherished childhood memories was the year we traveled by train from Tampa to Memphis. The journey was a new adventure for the Cicciaro family as we witnessed the landscape change before our eyes and anticipated spending time with relatives—ones who loved to have lots of fun.

On Christmas Eve, my dad dressed up in a Santa suit and went with Uncle Ted throughout the neighborhood. They arrived unannounced at several church members' homes to make sure all the children were getting ready for bed, much to the shock of the parents! Upon their return, we drank hot chocolate, ate Christmas sugar cookies, and laughed at their adventures.

To this day, the smell of cocoa and cookies baking takes me back to that trip and the impact it had upon our families. The inheritance created by family traditions and time spent together is an impermeable bond forged in love—and one that only gets stronger with time. ❋

TO THIS DAY, THE SMELL OF COCOA AND COOKIES BAKING TAKES ME BACK . . .

EMILY SUTHERLAND
Your Own Personal Christmas Potpourri

One night around Christmastime, I burned something in the kitchen. I think it was green beans . . . but whatever it was, it didn't smell festive. At all!

By necessity, I discovered a great way to create wonderful Christmas smells in a hurry: I whipped up my own simmering potpourri with things I already had on hand. It worked out so well, I started making potpourri even when I hadn't burned dinner!

It's really easy. You can use the peel from an orange or lemon (I now routinely save my orange peelings in a brown paper sack for potpourri later), or toss in a handful of cranberries or apple slices if you like, then add your favorite ingredients such as a little vanilla, or a few cloves or cinnamon sticks. You could even simmer some of those pesky pine needles that fall on the floor if you prefer the smell of pine over fruit and spices.

Simmer your custom collection of aromas on low heat in an uncovered pot or slow cooker filled with water. In addition to the wonderful fragrances that start to permeate your home, the steam will provide a bit of extra humidity in the house and soothe your nose from the dry winter air. (For safety's sake, check the water often and refill it if it gets low.)

For a delicious "drinkable potpourri," you can create a wonderful cranberry tea by filling a slow cooker with four cups of water, four tea bags, a quart or so of cranberry juice, orange and/or lemon slices, a few sprinkles of brown sugar if you wish, and a couple of cinnamon sticks or cloves. As soon as you begin to smell the wonderful combination, you know it's warm enough to drink. Then get your cup quick...before the kids come running! ❋

WES HAMPTON
The Smell of Christmas Morning

One of the smells (and tastes) that I always associate with Christmas is that of my mom's homemade sausage balls. I remember walking down the creaky steps in our charming old house every Christmas morning around 6:30. Yes, my brothers and I were early risers.

I knew it was officially Christmas Day once that aroma filled our house. The smell of those little morsels takes me back to my childhood every single time. ❋

SUSAN PECK-JACKSON
Christmas Breakfast

Christmas has always been my favorite time of the year. Mama made Christmas special with presents, music, and food, but most of all by sharing stories about the birth of Jesus Christ.

I still remember the smell of Christmas breakfast and the excitement that the morning brought to my life. Waking up on Christmas morning, I could smell bacon, eggs, biscuits, and gravy cooking throughout the house. And I couldn't wait to see what Santa brought me.

Now that I am grown and have a child of my own, I and my husband, David, share stories about the birth of Jesus Christ with our son, Joseph. I cook bacon, eggs, biscuits, and gravy on Christmas morning, and I am just as excited as Joseph is when he opens his presents. ❄

KAREN PECK-GOOCH
The Sweet Smell of Baby Boo

Mama and Daddy always made a big deal out of Christmas. My sisters and I were taught that the birth of Jesus was the main reason for celebrating Christmas. However, our parents always made sure that, while we were sleeping, "Santa Claus" would visit our home on Christmas Eve. We could choose three things that we wanted him to bring us.

Every year I would choose a baby doll as one of my three items. It was a big deal for me to pick the right doll. One particular year I chose the doll that became part of my life forever. She was my all-time favorite—the doll above all other dolls. When I saw her on the TV commercial, it was love at first sight! Her name was Baby Boo. After laying her down to sleep, she (with the help of batteries) would

open her eyes and cry. I could not wait to find Santa and ask him to special-deliver Baby Boo to my house.

Little did I know that a few days before Christmas, Santa and his entire workshop would come to my hometown. On our town square, the local TV cable channel was shooting live footage of cute little excited kids screaming out their requests while sitting on Santa's knee. While standing in the long line, I felt anxiety starting to creep in on me—I had never been on TV before. When I finally made it inside Santa's workshop, I climbed onto his knee and made a huge mistake: I looked at the TV monitor, saw myself—and

Karen Peck-Gooch holding Baby Boo and remembering the scent that takes her back to one very special Christmas morning.

completely froze! Honestly, I could not remember anything.

When Santa asked me what I wanted for Christmas, I just stared at him. My mind went blank. When I climbed down from his knee, a quick moment of sanity came back just in time for me to blurt out, "I want a doll!" Couldn't even remember her name.

I cried all the way home. How would Santa know which doll? Mama and Daddy assured me he would know.

I can't begin to express my happiness that particular Christmas morning when I saw Baby Boo sitting under the tree! She had a new plastic smell that I remember to this day. Every year at Christmastime, when I walk through the toy departments, sometimes I will get a whiff of that plastic smell and my mind will wander back to my Baby Boo . . . and I smile. ❋

SMELL *the* MEMORIES

CANDY CHRISTMAS
Ham for the Holidays

Have you ever encountered a familiar fragrance that tantalizes all your senses, and you suddenly find yourself taken back to another time? That is invariably my experience when I smell a ham baking in the oven.

No one could prepare a ham quite like my mother did for the Christmas holidays. She'd bake it for hours, its aroma filling the house until you could almost taste it. I remember one such ham that my mother prepared prior to a Christmas trip our family was taking to my Grandma Gussie's house some six hours away. Although Mother knew Grandma was making a Christmas feast, my mother never liked to go anywhere empty-handed. Her plan was to fully cook the ham, wrap it well, and secure it in the trunk of our car with all of the luggage and presents. She took great pains to score the ham prettily and colorfully decorate it in golden pineapple rings with plump red cherries in the center of each. It was spectacular!

We packed our gifts and belongings into the car and drove off, with the thrill of the journey happily guiding our chatter. Yet almost at once the conversation ceased as the

aroma of the succulent ham filled the car and dominated our thoughts. Dad steered the car onto the shoulder of the road, hopped out, and flung open the trunk. With Mom's permission, he carved a tiny piece of the ham from an obscure section with his pocketknife, closed the trunk, and returned to evenly divide the tiny morsel between us all. Then we drove on.

Of course, this didn't make that luscious aroma fade. Nor did it satisfy our cravings. Soon we succumbed again . . . and again . . . until all that was left of mother's fabulous ham was the bone! ❋

WESLEY PRITCHARD
Teaberry

When I was a kid, we would always go back to the mountains of North Carolina at Christmastime to be with our family and see my grandma. My grandma, Edith Haas, directed the choir at Bethel Church until she was in her eighties. She went home to be with the Lord last year at ninety-three.

Each year Grandma took all of us grandchildren up into the mountains to search for wild teaberry. She would find it for us and we would pick it, kind of wipe it off, and chew the leaves. It tasted so good to us! It was a small thing, I guess, but to me it was so amazing to pick something out of the ground and chew it.

Grandma always took us to church and would give us gum. You could smell it in her purse—Teaberry gum! To this day

Wesley Pritchard with his grandma, Edith Haas.

OUR OWN
Frankincense
~ *Calvin Miller* ~

In that not-so-long-ago world
where Grandma made raspberry jam,
Grandpa chopped the wood.
Because of his good axe,
we could smell Christmas.
We knew the warming smell of hickory logs
cast into the pot-bellied stove.
It warmed our lungs as it warmed our hands,
and glorious was its smell.
Our Christmas tree
was also Grandpa's gift for the season.
He searched the snowy woods
until he came across a thick cedar tree
that would fit into the living room.
And when he found it, the delight
of his own kind of frankincense came to be.
He swung the axe that hacked its way
through the gray bark
till the flying chips of cedar,
still fresh and damp with frost,
filled his nostrils.
Then he brought the axe-hewn
Christmas tree home to us.
Cedar, I tell you, was his glorious gift to us—
that combination of sweet sap
and near cherry wood
that lines a bridal chest
was most divinely spent on human nostrils.

Continued on page 122

when I walk into a Cracker Barrel (which is probably the only place that sells it), I don't smell the chicken or the meatloaf . . . I smell Teaberry gum. They keep it right by the counter, and it immediately brings me back to Christmas in the woods with my Grandma. I miss her and love her so much. ❄

Snapping green beans with George Younce took Ernie Haase back many years to the smell of green beans cooking for Christmas dinner at his grandparents' house.

ERNIE HAASE
The Smell of Green Beans

Christmas is so full of great smells, but there is one that I'm especially fond of. Whenever I smell green beans cooking back in the big kettle pot on the stove —not the fancy ones that snap but the kind with fat—I think of my grandma. During the summers, I used to help her and my grandpa pick, snap, and clean those beans, and I love the memory of doing that. So when the smell of green beans cooking makes its way through the house before Christmas dinner, I am immediately transported back in time and see myself on the porch with my grandparents, talking about nothing as we snapped those green beans.

I remember years later, after I told George Younce that story, he took me to the market and we got some green beans to snap. Now, when I smell green beans, I think of my grandma *and* George!

Christmas is a great time of year, and it becomes even more precious when we have special ways of remembering the people we love. ❄

SQUIRE PARSONS
The Smell of Oranges

I went into a studio one day to record an album, and I had put some oranges in my satchel. As we were listening to one of the playbacks, I pulled out an orange and started to peel it, and one of the musicians spoke up and said, "It smells like Christmas!"

That started a whole conversation, and we all began talking about how oranges always make us think of Christmas. When I was growing up, I don't remember having much fresh fruit throughout the year. We raised our own organic food (before we knew that was cool), but Dad would always purchase a crate of oranges at Christmas.

Still today, whenever I eat an orange, I think, *Mmm! Smells like Christmas!* ❄

COMBINATIONS *that* "SMELL LIKE CHRISTMAS"

A smell like washing day! That was the cloth.
A smell like an eating-house and a pastry cook
Next door to each other,
With a laundress's next door to that!
That was the pudding!

CHARLES DICKENS
A CHRISTMAS CAROL

BUDDY GREENE
Inhaling Christmas

I associate Christmas not just with one smell, but a certain combination of smells all going on together. We always get a real tree, and we clip evergreen to put on the mantle. So that aroma combines with the smell of our wood-burning fireplace, candles, popcorn, some kind of potpourri simmering, and my personal favorite: brownies or chocolate chip cookies baking. All these things together smell like Christmas to me.

Our experiences and memories are all dependent on the senses, but that's particularly true at this time of year. After all, the story of Jesus is all about God inhabiting the material world. This is what separates Christianity from other religions of the world. It's about spirit and body and how they are inseparable. So to breathe in all the things that remind us of Christmas is to make Christmas a part of us.

Man-made holidays are fun and everything, but they tend to get old. Every time Christmas comes around, though, we are ready to experience it all new again. We never get tired of it! And I imagine I will never get tired of smelling brownies

baking in the oven and all those other things that remind me it's time to celebrate! ❋

GORDON MOTE
Smelling the Candlelight Service

There are certain candles Kimberly only burns during the weeks between Thanksgiving and Christmas. At that time, even the outside air in our neighborhood smells different! When we take walks during the Christmas season, there are more aromas than usual—neighbors are baking; more fires are burning in fireplaces. There is so much more to take in during Christmas than during any other season.

One vivid memory I have is the smell of the candlelight service on Christmas Eve. The smell of the church and of the Christmas tree (our church always gets a live

Our Own
Frankincense
~ Calvin Miller ~

But Grandpa's cedar only
challenged Grandma's ingenuity.
Not to be outdone,
Grandma's food was there,
her own kind of frankincense
luring our hearts right after
it captured our noses.
The smell of cranberries simmering.
Popcorn popping in
a thousand small explosions,
only to face the needled thread
that turned it into garlands for
Grandpa's cedar tree.
Did I mention pies
and bread and giblet stuffing
and minted cocoa?
And the fragrance of
sweet bleach in the sheets where
we slept and
dreamed of Christmas morning?
We drew in such deep draughts of
December's scented air,
we did not breathe it out again
till January.

tree) combined with the smell of candle wax . . . nowhere else in the world have I ever experienced that particular combination. Then, at the end of the service, everyone blows out their candles. It's a specific, smoky scent that means it's Christmas Eve, and time to go home and celebrate with my family. ❈

JOYCE MARTIN
Oranges and Cloves

There are a lot of smells that I associate with Christmas—the smell of the fresh-cut tree, of popcorn popping, of hot cocoa—but my favorite is cloves and oranges. I am not sure where my mom got the idea, but she would bring home from the store oranges bundled in red netting and a jar of whole cloves. She would lay them all out on the table, and we would start the process of poking the cloves into the oranges until they were almost covered. Then we would put the red netting back over them like little packages and scatter them throughout the house. We even gave some away as gifts.

With every piercing of that clove into that orange skin, the combination of those two scents would fill the room. It smelled like Christmas to me. ❈

BILL GAITHER
Incense and Manure

As an Indiana kid who grew up on a farm, we always had to get the chores done early on Christmas before we could celebrate. The smell of the barn—that unique combination of hay and manure—was an aroma I knew well, and pushing hay from up in the hay mow down into the manger for the animals

to feed on was a part of my regular routine. So early in life, the smells of the barn gave me a very real understanding of the story of Jesus' birth.

Many years later, I enjoyed a very different Christmas experience that brought the season to life in a completely different way. I attended the Festival of Lessons and Carols at Sewanee University, an Episcopal school in Tennessee. They host this annual, liturgical Christmas service based on one that originated in 1918 at King's College Chapel in Cambridge, England.

The chapel was lit only with candles, everyone sang carols, readings were recited from Scripture . . . But the most unforgettable thing about that beautiful service was the sweet smell of incense that filled the room! For this farm kid who had always associated the story of Christ's birth with the smell of hay and manure, this was an entirely new experience! I never wanted to become Episcopalian so badly!

I think many evangelical churches over the years have been missing out on one of the scents of Christmas: the incense that is the symbol of our songs and prayers, our deepest longings and highest praise ascending to the Father. I think this makes His great heart glad.

I'm thankful for the broad spectrum of experiences that have allowed me to appreciate—with my nose, of all things—the humility into which Christ was born, as well as the incredibly lavish fragrances that, like the wise men, we bring as our best gifts to the King. ❄

Bill (left) and his little brother Danny grew up very familiar with the smells of a stable like the one in which Jesus was born.

The Taste
OF CHRISTMAS

✳ ✳ ✳

This is the season to
throw diet to the winds and
eat our way through.

merica truly is the great melting pot; the foods of all our various heritages have marched right onto the Christmas table, bringing us back to our roots while, at the same time, making each family's celebration unique.

Italian families may add pastas and fabulous sauces to the Christmas menu, while Swedish families insist on including gubböra (an egg and anchovy mixture), vörtbröd (a rye bread), and lutfisk to the traditional ham and potatoes. For Irish descendants, potatoes are not optional, and soda bread will be a staple as well. A breakfast favorite of the South that has made its way to us via France is "chocolate pudding" over homemade biscuits.

Whatever our family histories might be, food is a vital part of Christmas. And kitchens are the place to gather, as fruitcakes, Christmas cookies, cream pies with meringue, mince tarts, turkeys, hams, roasts, winter vegetables, and special breads are pulled from the ovens or simmer on the stove.

Some of the best gifts of the season are those from the kitchen. Baked goods wrapped in colorful boxes; homemade, canned jellies, jams, and chutneys; delicious breads and pies—all are sure to get grateful responses from neighbors, mail carriers, teachers, and business associates.

Some of my favorite tastes of Christmas are those sipped steaming-hot from a mug or cup: hot chocolate, wassail, rich coffees, chai or Christmas teas, and warmed fruit juices and punches. At our house, we have a golden yellow earthenware pitcher and a set of gigantic, matching cups and saucers lettered on the sides with the word *chocolat*. This special beverage set is saved for one purpose: hot chocolate with a melting marshmallow for children who come in half-frozen from sledding on the hillside.

As I think of it, Christmas is a giant, season-long tasting party. From home to home and family to family, we find ways to say: "Christmas is love. Taste and see!"

Gloria Gaither

Taste AND *See*
~ *Calvin Miller* ~

First, come with me to the wonder of . . .

rustic shepherds

kneeling in a shepherd's cave.

Then come with me to Grandma's house.

Here is a jar of raspberry jam

next to a loaf of her best bread.

And there is Grandma, this wonderful,

aged lover of God,

a kind of angel who wanted nothing

more than to see her children and

grandchildren love God.

And along the way, while she prayed

hour by hour

that all of us children would please

the Christ of Bethlehem,

she stirred some of God's rich raspberries

into pectin and sugar, thinking

all the time of her

Christmas Day breakfast.

And while the glorious confection was

hot and red,

she stirred the whole thing into a Mason jar,

sterilized the joy in boiling water—

the rubber seal melting onto a glass rim—

and the jam cooled and waited.

Waited and waited.

Continued on page 135

CHRISTMAS FEASTING

*"Gifts of time and love
are surely the basic ingredients of
a truly merry Christmas. "*

PEG BRACKEN

LILY ISAACS
My First Taste of Christmas

Being raised in a Jewish home, we celebrated Hanukkah rather than Christmas. This holiday has nothing to do with Christmas, but somehow it always seemed to fall at about the same time of year. It kind of distracted me from feeling left out, because we would light the menorah for eight days and exchange some gifts with family and friends. We also had macaroons—a family favorite—and a special Hanukkah pastry called rougallach, which my mother made.

In college I majored in theater arts and took a summer course one year at Carnegie Tech in Pittsburgh, where I met my roommate, a girl named Maria Neumann. Her family lived in

Manhattan. Her mother was a famous ballerina, and her father was also in show business.

Maria and I became best of friends almost immediately. She, like myself, was studying acting and was also a folk singer. We began singing together in the dorm and continued when we went back to the city . . . and we somehow landed a recording contract with Columbia Records and started performing all over Greenwich Village. It was a very exciting part of my life—and the time when I first got a taste of Christmas. Literally!

The first Christmas I really experienced was when Maria and her family invited my brother and me to their home for a Christmas dinner party. I will never forget getting on a subway in the Bronx on the way to Manhattan with my brother, Hy. It was already snowing that evening, and it was extremely cold. Yet we were so excited that the cold didn't matter. When we finally arrived at Maria's family's apartment, the smell of fresh bread and cider and cinnamon put me in a trance! We walked in and saw holly everywhere, along with mistletoe and poinsettias and the most amazing Christmas tree! It was overwhelming, and they made us feel so welcome.

We met some other guests and ate a big meal with turkey and ham with all the trimmings. After dinner we were served

Lily is pictured here with her dear college friend, Maria Neumann, who helped give Lily her first real taste of Christmas.

eggnog. We spent the night there and woke up the next morning to coffee and fresh cinnamon rolls. What a wonderful time we had! I will never forget that first Christmas. The memory is embedded in my heart forever.

Now, years after that first Christmas celebration, the Isaacs' Christmas dinner is always followed by this family tradition— taking turns reading the story of the first Christmas.

Now my favorite family Christmas tradition of ours is the reading of the real Christmas story—the birth of our Lord Jesus. First we have dinner, which usually consists of lasagna, salad, garlic bread, and hot apple pie. Then we gather in my family room. I have five grandchildren, and of course with my three kids and their spouses, there's a bunch of us! We sit around in a big circle, and all five of my brilliant grandchildren take turns passing the Bible around, with each one reading a passage of Scripture. Next, we all take turns and tell how grateful we are to be together and how we praise the Lord for His gift of life to us. We then get down on our knees in a circle and have a family prayer. This is the most precious time for me. The meal, the presents—none of the hoopla even comes close to the specialness of this time together. But it all started the year I was invited to the Christmas feast of my dear friend and her family. ✳

"When it comes to the tastes of Christmas,
so much comes to mind: oranges from my sister in Florida,
homemade caramels, eggnog, hot drinks like cider, tea,
and flavored coffees, and Christmas morning brunch!
I easily gain five pounds every year."

BUDDY GREENE

GLORIA GAITHER
Christmas Breakfast at the Gaithers'

"Carolers on our kitchen island make me smile when I'm working at the stove." —Gloria

The only time of the whole year that I make chipped beef gravy and biscuits is Christmas morning. The whole family crowds around our big oak table by the kitchen fire (which Bill keeps burning all night Christmas Eve), and there is much happy conversation and story-telling. With the gravy and biscuits I usually serve fresh fruit (berries, melon, mandarin oranges, bananas) in glasses I've chilled in the freezer, and a big plate of scrambled eggs sprinkled with grated cheddar. When the children were home, this breakfast followed the reading of the Christmas story from Luke 2 and the opening of gifts, but now that they open Christmas presents earlier, in their own homes, they all come over afterward for breakfast around 10 a.m. The children bring favorite things to show us, and the conversation is about the great things that happened in their own houses when they awoke on Christmas morning. After breakfast, we gather in the living room with our last cup of coffee or juice and open presents from each other and the friends we've added and, thankfully, great-grandparents and cousins who drop by. ✳

CHIPPED BEEF GRAVY

2 (4.5-ounce) jars of dried beef
(I use the Armour® brand)

¼ stick of butter

1 cup scalding hot water

2 cups milk

2 heaping tablespoons flour

pepper

1. With kitchen shears, cut beef in narrow strips into a large skillet.

2. Add butter and water, bring to a boil, cover, and reduce heat to a simmer for 10 minutes to coax the flavor from the meat. Add pepper.

3. Meanwhile, put milk and flour into a shaker, and shake until smooth.

4. Gradually add flour mixture to meat mixture over medium heat, stirring constantly. Have extra milk on hand to thin if gravy thickens beyond the consistency of a creamy sauce.

5. Add more pepper if desired (you are not likely to need salt, as the dried beef is salty). Serve in a Christmas tureen with stacks of hot, homemade biscuits.

GLORIA'S PERFECT BISCUITS EVERY TIME!

2 cups flour

4 teaspoons baking powder

1½ teaspoons salt

½ cup shortening
(I use butter-flavored Crisco®)

1 egg

milk

1. In a large mixing bowl, combine flour, baking powder, and salt. Work in the shortening.

2. Break the egg in a cup and fill the rest of the cup with milk. Pour milk and egg into flour-and-shortening mixture, and mix until all ingredients are just blended. Don't overmix.

3. Pour dough onto a floured cutting board and gently shape with floured hands until dough is about 1-inch thick. Cut with biscuit cutter and place biscuits in a greased, 9-inch cake pan. Keep gently tucking the edges of the remaining dough into shape, but don't handle any more than needed.

4. Bake biscuits in oven at 350° until lightly golden brown. Serve hot with butter and honey, or with chipped beef or sausage gravy.

SOLVEIG LEITHAUG
Christmas Dinner: from Norway to Nashville

Christmas was a season filled with traditions. Mom would start baking her seven kinds of Christmas cookies early in December. The Christmas tree was always freshly cut and decorated on what we would call Little Christmas Eve, December 23rd. In Norway we celebrate Christmas Eve as our "big day," with the rice porridge served at lunch with a hidden almond. (Whoever gets the almond in their bowl wins the treasured, pig-shaped marzipan.) Churches all over the country would offer multiple Christmas services into the late afternoon, then everyone, festively dressed, would eat their Christmas dinners and open up gifts in the evening.

Dinner would then be served piping hot, right after the church bells rang in Christmas. The traditional west coast Christmas meal of smoked rack of lamb ribs (*pinnekjøtt*) was served with the standard side dishes of steamed potatoes, carrots, and mashed rutabagas, drizzled with drippings of bacon as an added touch. Mom always added a few *raspeballer*, or potato dumplings, as well—one of my all-time favorite dishes.

Kransekake is a traditional Norwegian almond ring cake, which is a Christmas favorite but can also be used for other special holidays. The most common dessert for a Norwegian Christmas dinner is *Multekrem*, or cloud berries with cream in *krumkake*, a crusty, thin, rolled sweet wafer like a cone-shaped cookie. Although Mom

Kransekake (left) is a traditional Norwegian almond ring cake, and also a Christmas favorite.

would make *Multekrem*, she more often served us her fresh fruit salad with nuts and finely chopped pieces of Norwegian chocolates accompanied by a dollop of vanilla ice cream or whipped cream.

Reading the Christmas story from Luke 2 in honor of our Savior's birth before enjoying our Christmas dinner is a tradition I have brought with me from my Nor-

The photo from our Christmas dinner table in Nashville: to the left are my sons David (18) and John (10), then my daughter Kari (16) and me. (Jim is the photographer.)

wegian family. It's something my children have grown up with—and something we have incorporated into our new life with my husband, Jim.

Mashed rutabagas is one of those dishes that we (kids included) will go back for a second and third time, until it is ALL gone. It is indeed a great accompaniment to any meat or poultry dish. When paired with cured lamb ribs, the combination is simply magic.

Jim "Big Chaff" Chaffee enjoying Christmas morning breakfast.

FLAVORFUL MASHED RUTABAGAS

*2-3 pounds rutabaga,
peeled and cut in chunks*

water

2 teaspoons salt

⅓ cup butter

*½ teaspoon
freshly ground black pepper*

1. Put the rutabagas in a large saucepan and cover with water. Add 1 teaspoon of salt. Bring to a boil; reduce heat, cover, and simmer for 25-30 minutes or until tender.

2. Drain and let dry in a colander or in the pan with the top ajar.

3. Mash the rutabagas with butter, stir in 1 teaspoon of salt, and sprinkle the black pepper. Serve immediately.

(SERVES 4 TO 6)

Options:

❋ A combination of rutabagas and carrots also works well (2/3 rutabagas, 1/3 carrots). At times I add 3-4 tablespoons of milk or half-and-half for a creamier consistency.

❋ Instead of cooking the rutabagas in salted water, chicken stock is a tasty option.

The following dish is part of a new tradition of tastes that have found their way into our Tennessee home. It is Jim's specialty, and it is a fresh, sweet and tangy substitute for the processed, canned cranberry sauce you get in the grocery store. It is also exceptionally tasty on your turkey sandwich late on Christmas night. *Bon appetit!* ❋

BIG CHAFF'S
HOLIDAY CRANBERRY RELISH

1 pound cranberries

1 apple

1 pear

2 oranges

1 cup sugar

1 lemon, juiced (optional)

4 ounces Cointreau® or Grand Marnier®

1. Very coarsely chop the cranberries in a food processor.

2. Manually chop the unskinned apple and pear into small cubes.

3. From the oranges, zest as much of the peel and squeeze as much of the juice as possible. Add Sugar.

4. Mix all ingredients together in a glass bowl until sugar is dissolved.

5. Allow flavors to blend for a minimum of 12 hours in the refrigerator, and freeze whatever you are not going to use right away.

JOY GARDNER
Our Family Feast

Every year our entire family gathers at our house for Christmas dinner. We each bring our favorite dish to contribute to what has become our traditional Christmas meal. I make beef tenderloin, butternut squash soufflé, and green beans with pine nuts. My sister, Joan, makes chocolate pies, coconut cream pies, and chocolate éclairs from recipes that have been passed down through our family. My son-in-law, Scott, makes the mashed potatoes and won't even tell us what he puts in them—probably because they are a heart attack waiting to happen! Our oldest daughter, Dionne, makes a sweet potato and apple casserole; my nieces Alyson and Elizabeth make corn pudding and roasted vegetables;

Pictured here by the Christmas tree is the Gardner family (left to right): Lauren, Landy, Joy, Dionne, and her husband, Scott, and their son, Dyson.

and when my brother and sister-in-law are able to join us, they always bring a gourmet surprise.

Lauren, our younger daughter, lived in France for several months while she was in college, and ever since then, she selects fine cheeses, fruits, preserves, and imported honey—a traditional French cheese-tasting—for us to enjoy on Christmas Eve after all the preparations for Christmas Day are complete. We usually conclude Christmas evening with our family playing games, watching the kids perform the plays they have written, and reminiscing about all the wonderful times we have spent celebrating the MOST wonderful time of the year. ❄

JOY GARDNER
Our Family Recipe

CHOCOLATE ÉCLAIRS

1 cup water

½ cup shortening (Crisco®)

⅛ teaspoon salt

1 cup flour

4 eggs

1. Put water, shortening, and salt into a pan and bring to a boil, making sure that shortening has melted.
2. Reduce heat to warm and add flour all at once. Stir well until it makes a ball around spoon.
3. Remove from heat and add eggs, one at a time, beating thoroughly after each egg.
4. Drop by tablespoon onto cookie sheet.
5. Bake at 425° for 20 minutes.
6. Reduce heat to 325° and bake 20 more minutes.
7. Allow puffs to cool.
8. Cut tops off and clean out some of the inside before filling with cooled filling. Replace tops, then finish with icing.

CUSTARD FILLING

Double this recipe if desired—I found I had to double the filling to have enough custard to fill the puffs.

¾ cups sugar

1½ cups milk

2 tablespoons flour

2 tablespoons butter

2 eggs

1 teaspoon vanilla

1. Combine ingredients and cook over medium heat, stirring constantly, until custard boils and thickens.
2. Add vanilla and beat well.

ICING

1 stick butter

3 tablespoons cocoa

6 tablespoons milk

1 box powdered sugar

1 teaspoon vanilla

1 cup pecans

1. Bring butter, cocoa, and milk to a boil and cook 1 minute.
2. Pour over powdered sugar, add vanilla, and beat well.
3. Add pecans.

The Christmas Treats

If we could but look for a moment or two
In all that heaven must be
We'd find it eternally brownies and cream
Delicious and calorie-free.

CALVIN MILLER
"THE YEAR-END DIET"

SQUIRE PARSONS
Chocolate-Covered Cherries

When I was growing up, we always got about four boxes of chocolate-covered cherries during the Christmas season. In fact, I was always getting in trouble for not leaving any for the rest of my family. Today, when I see the store displays go up with boxes and boxes of those chocolate-covered cherries, I know Christmas has arrived! ❆

GLORIA GAITHER
Gaither Welcome Wassail

Nothing smells better when guests walk in out of the December cold than the smell of apple cider and spices perking in the kitchen. And nothing tastes so "welcome" as a sip of steaming wassail from a glass mug with a cinnamon stick floating on the top.

I make this recipe in my big 36-cup silver percolator; that way, a houseful of company can return again and again for refills all evening. The kids love it too, after an afternoon of sledding on the hillside or ice-skating on the pond. ❆

Gaither Welcome Wassail offers a warm and welcoming treat after an afternoon of sledding.

GAITHER WELCOME WASSAIL

❆ In a 36-cup percolator, add:

1 gallon apple cider

1 (32-ounce) bottle cranberry juice

❆ In percolator basket, place:

½ lemon, scored and cut into pieces

6-8 cinnamon sticks

10-12 whole cloves

6-8 whole allspice

optional: 1 teaspoon rum flavoring

❆ Plug in and perk as usual. Serve with a cinnamon stick in each cup.

BEN ISAACS
Chocolate and Candy Canes

I think my favorite Christmas memory would be going to my grandparents'—my dad's parents—in Kentucky and someone delivering a fifty-five-gallon barrel of chocolate. They put it on the porch, and we kids would go out there with spoons and just break off chocolate and eat it. I will never forget it—it was good chocolate! I don't know where it came from.

My grandparents didn't have electricity, and they were very poor. They were farmers, and I don't ever remember receiving any gifts from them for Christmas. Of course, when they died, there were over 100 grandchildren! My dad was the baby of seventeen children, so for them to get something like that barrel of chocolate and let us grandchildren enjoy it . . . You can imagine probably twenty kids and the fifty-five-gallon barrel of chocolate. It's a smile in my memory!

Another thing my grandparents would do is bust up candy canes. People would bring my grandparents big old candy canes. When I was a kid, those candy canes looked as big as my leg, but they were probably five-pound candy canes. And there was always a hammer sitting there on the kitchen counter, and all of us would just bust off a piece of the candy and eat it whenever we wanted. So every time I eat chocolate or peppermint now, I think about those days visiting my grandparents for Christmas. ❋

REGGIE SMITH
The Taste of Fudge

My dad was the music director and Mom played the organ for our church, so we all participated in the annual Christmas cantata two weeks before Christmas. On Sunday night after the cantata, we would join several other families and go caroling to the shut-ins who could not make it to the cantata. All the folks we visited were so kind and appreciative, but there was one particular house we would always save for last—the Norris' house. Every year after we finished singing for them, they would invite us inside for homemade fudge! Mrs. Norris handmade every flavor of fudge you could ever want—chocolate, peanut butter, walnut, chocolate and pecan—along with Martha Washington candy. It was incredible! The moment I tasted that fudge, I knew Christmas had arrived!

The Norrises have since passed away, but I still remember that ex-

GRANDMA ISAACS HAD SEVENTEEN CHILDREN AND MORE THAN A HUNDRED GRANDCHILDREN! SHE AND GRANDPA ISAACS TREATED THEM ALL TO CHOCOLATE AND CANDY CANES AT CHRISTMAS.

perience so vividly! And I still associate the taste of fudge with the start of Christmas! ❄

JASON CRABB
Peanut Butter Fudge

I always call my mother-in-law, Shelta Reno, when we are going over to her house for Christmas: "Don't forget the peanut butter fudge." She makes the best peanut butter fudge on the planet! She always fixes us a big pan of it . . . like I need it! I'd do a whole lot better without it, but that's one thing that I look forward to—a big glass of milk and that peanut butter fudge she makes. ❄

Taste AND *See*
~ *Calvin Miller* ~

Later the trees gave up their leaves,
the snow came,
and Grandma praised the Christ who had
made her life whole,
who had sanctified the season of Advent.
She lit the candles and waited
with a Christmas carol on her lips.
And at long last, the day came. Deck the halls!
The raspberries were still as red as
the church's altar cloth—
a testament of her love for her family.
She was singing "Away in a Manger"
(it's every grandmother's favorite, I dare say)
as she took the steaming loaf of
bread from her oven.
And then she studied
the fruit of her summer's labor.
Long months earlier,
while she'd hummed a summer hymn,
She'd thought of this very day
When her family, ever at the top of her prayers,
Would be gathered to read
the old birth story from Luke.
Then they would pray;
then they would laugh and enjoy
the season as God intended.

Continued on page 142

ANTHONY BURGER
Old-Fashioned Potato Candy

Anthony's mom makes this candy every holiday season. ❋

OLD-FASHIONED POTATO CANDY

1 small potato
(the size of an egg
or as close to it as possible)

1 pound box of confectioner's sugar, sifted

peanut butter, any kind

1. Boil potato in water until completely cooked. Then, while the potato is still hot, peel it and mash it in a large bowl. (You can choose to peel the potato prior to cooking if you wish.)

2. Immediately add all the sugar and knead into dough. Roll into either a thin circle or rectangle onto wax paper.

3. Spread a thin layer of peanut butter over dough. Roll it up as you would roll a jelly roll.

4. Wrap in waxed paper and chill in the refrigerator for 30 minutes.

5. Slice and store in an air-tight container. (You may store in the refrigerator if you wish.)

GORDON MOTE
Aunt Martha's Chocolate Fudge

This recipe has been in my family for over thirty-five years, and Aunt Martha still makes it every Christmas. Christmas wouldn't be the same without it. ❋

MARTHA'S FUDGE

5 cups sugar

1 large can condensed milk

2 sticks of margarine

3 packages chocolate chips
(1 milk chocolate, 2 dark chocolate)

1 large jar marshmallow cream

2 tablespoons vanilla

2 cups chopped pecans
*(*more for Gordon, none for Samantha)*

1. Bring sugar, condensed milk, and margarine to a boil in a pan, then cook for 9 minutes on low heat, stirring constantly.

2. Remove from heat, and add chocolate chips, marshmallow cream, vanilla, and nuts. Beat with large mixer until hard enough to pour.

3. Allow to cool, then cut into squares. Makes approximately 5 pounds.

MARK LOWRY
Grandma's Special Jell-O

When I was a kid, Christmas was all about the gifts. My dad didn't grow up with a lot—he would get an orange for Christmas as a kid—so when he became an attorney and was able to live comfortably, our Christmases were ridiculous! They were full of toys and games and wonderful things . . . It was actually a lot about excess. And our family has carried on the tradition. (It's hard not to in these days of commercialism.)

But one of the things that speaks most to me about Christmas is something a lot simpler—my grandpa's Jell-O. Actually, my grandma made it for him. It was a green Jell-O, and we had it every Christmas. It was amazing, filled with pecans and cottage cheese and pineapples—all in a Pyrex pan . . . Yum! That Jell-O was a delicious reminder that it was time to get out the tree and really begin the Christmas season. ❊

ANDY ANDREWS
Birthday Cake and Homegrown Oranges

When I was growing up, Christmas Eve at our house was always the time for Jesus' birthday party, complete with a cake. This is still a tradition every year at my house. It keeps

The Andrews boys are ready to deliver this basket of homegrown citrus fruit to their neighbors.

our thoughts on the reason for the season. Adam (8) and Austin (11) really look forward to the party. We also always give our neighbors something from our house that we have made or grown. ❋

JANET PASCHAL
Italian Cream Cake

ITALIAN CREAM CAKE

5 eggs,
with whites and yolks separated
½ cup shortening
½ cup margarine (1 stick)
2 cups sugar

1 cup buttermilk

1 teaspoon soda

½ teaspoon salt

2 cups flour

1 teaspoon vanilla

2 cups coconut

1 cup pecans, chopped

1 cup maraschino cherries, chopped

1. Beat egg whites in large bowl and set aside.

2. Cream shortening, margarine, and sugar. Add egg yolks one at a time, and cream well.

3. Add buttermilk alternately with combined dry ingredients. Stir in vanilla.

4. Add coconut, pecans, and cherries.

5. Fold in stiffly beaten egg whites.

6. Bake at 350° in three-layer cake pans or a 13 x 9 cake pan for 40 minutes.

FROSTING

½ cup margarine (1 stick)
at room temperature

1 (8-ounce) package cream cheese
at room temperature

1 cup pecans, chopped

1 pound powdered sugar

1 teaspoon vanilla

maraschino cherries, chopped

Combine all ingredients and frost cooled cake. Cake freezes beautifully, too!

Christmas Cookies

ICING

Mix together:

2 cups confectioner's sugar

1 teaspoon vanilla

3 tablespoons cold water

ERNIE & LISA HAASE
Silver Bells

SILVER BELLS

1 cup butter (2 sticks), softened

½ cup confectioner's sugar

1 teaspoon vanilla

¼ teaspoon salt

2¼ cups all-purpose flour

1. Preheat oven to 375°.

2. Mix butter, sugar, vanilla, and salt. Stir in flour. Use hands to mix.

3. Take dough in small chunks and flatten on wax paper. Use a cookie cutter to create bell shapes in dough, then place on cookie sheet.

4. Bake 10-12 minutes, then let cool slightly before removing with a knife or small spatula.

GORDON MOTE
Neiman-Marcus Cookies

At the Mote house, we always know Christmas is near when Kimberly bakes Neiman-Marcus cookies. She only makes them during Christmastime, and it's usually while the rest of us are watching a Christmas movie like *A Christmas Story* or *Miracle on 34th Street*. (We wait to watch *It's a Wonderful Life* until a time when she isn't baking, because that's her favorite Christmas movie.)

Soon after we start smelling these cookies, she comes in with a big tray of them hot out of the oven. They're almost as big as your hand! We can hardly bite into them without burning our mouths because they're so hot—but they're so good we can't wait! ❄

NEIMAN-MARCUS COOKIES
(NEIMANMARCUS.COM)

½ cup butter (1 stick), softened

1 cup light brown sugar

3 tablespoons granulated sugar

1 large egg

2 teaspoons vanilla extract

1¾ cups all-purpose flour

½ teaspoon baking powder

½ teaspoon baking soda

½ teaspoon salt

1½ teaspoons instant espresso coffee powder

1½ cups semi-sweet chocolate chips

1. Preheat oven to 300°. Cream butter with the sugars using an electric mixer on medium speed until fluffy (approximately 30 seconds).

2. Beat in egg and vanilla extract for another 30 seconds.

3. In a mixing bowl, sift together dry ingredients and beat into the butter mixture at low speed for about 15 seconds. Stir in espresso coffee powder and chocolate chips.

4. Using a 1-ounce scoop or a 2-tablespoon measure, drop cookies onto greased cookie sheet about 3 inches apart. Gently press down on dough with back of a spoon to spread out into a 2-inch circle.

5. Bake for about 20 minutes or until nicely browned around the edges. Bake a little longer for a crispier cookie.

Yields 2 dozen cookies

Our Christmas Heritage table, with a family picture at each place-setting for recalling treasured memories. The centerpiece recalls vocations and hobbies of those we loved.

BILL & GLORIA GAITHER
Setting the Table to Remember the Past

Someone has so rightly stated that those who don't know where they came from usually don't know where they are going. As we look to a new year and a fresh start, Christmas is the perfect time not only to remember together the birth of our Savior, who came to clear up any misconceptions we might have about what God is like, but to remember those who have preceded us in our life and faith journeys.

Simply framed photos of the matriarchs and patriarchs of our families make intriguing Christmas dinner placecards, each with a short description of the subject's interests, hobbies, gifts, and personality. A table centerpiece of traditional Christmas greenery and ornaments can be made more meaningful and interesting by including symbols such as small garden tools, sewing necessities, art supplies, knitting or crocheting items, etc., that help make each ancestor "come to life" for the younger generation that might not have had a chance to know them. The photos and symbols make irresistible story starters for table conversation.

Including tales of funny incidents, along with the person's quirks, accomplishments,

and even failures will refresh the memories of those who knew these relatives, while at the same time helping the younger generation understand them as real people who played a role in who they themselves have become. The kids can then choose the person they would most like to have known and tell what they would like to have asked him or her.

Central to this celebration of "Christmas Past" is a discussion of the Christ Child and what He grew up to do for the whole world, and our families in particular—redeeming our failures, healing our wounds, and filling our days with life abundant. It is because of Him, after all, that we are together around this table on this day. ❄

CHRISTMAS IS
THE PERFECT TIME NOT ONLY
TO REMEMBER TOGETHER
THE BIRTH OF OUR SAVIOR...
BUT TO REMEMBER
THOSE WHO HAVE PRECEDED US
IN OUR LIFE
AND FAITH JOURNEYS.

MOTHER'S SOFT MOLASSES COOKIES

These cookies are incredible with tea, milk, or good coffee.

1 cup natural dark molasses

1 cup brown sugar, packed down

1 cup melted butter

4 cups flour (just a bit less)

1 teaspoon each of the following:

baking soda

allspice

cinnamon

mace

cloves

nutmeg

ginger

salt

*1 cup pecans or
English walnuts, chopped*

1. In mixing bowl, slowly mix molasses, brown sugar, and melted butter.

2. Slowly add flour and sprinkle in spices. Mix together.

3. Fold in chopped nuts.

Taste AND *See*
~ *Calvin Miller* ~

As this matriarch of her Christian family
pried open with a butter knife
The single seal of a simple Mason jar. . .
a glorious Christmas ritual was born
in every corner of their senses.
The vacuum pop of the jam jar greeted their ears
like an alleluia rising from Luke 2.
The outrush of sugar and raspberries
inebriated our senses like the incense,
the myrrh of ancient kings.
The sticky feel of red jam on a wooden spoon
like the scarlet pomegranates of Jordan
begging the tongue to taste and marvel,
The sight of scarlet berries
shining through the glass
as vivid as starlight on a shepherd's crook.

Can we so easily write raspberries
into the Nativity of the Son of God?
Bring your soul to worship with me
While I celebrate all the Christmas gifts.
Open your nervous system till all five of your
Senses meet on an ancient hillside.
Then be still, very still,
Till your eyes see, Your ears hear,
Your nose can catch the whiff of heaven's incense,
Your tongue tastes the figs of a starlit bush,
Your fingers touch mystic locks of angel's hair.
Then tell me,
Is anything not sacred in an old woman's family?

Continued on page 147

4. Divide into three portions and roll into logs about 2 inches in diameter. Wrap each in plastic wrap and chill at least 1 hour. (Dough may be kept longer.)

5. Slice dough in ½-inch thick sections and bake at 350°. (Don't overbake.)

6. Cool and store in sealed plastic container between layers of wax paper.

PECAN PUFFS

These are beautiful for gifts at Christmas.

1 cup shortening

1½ cups confectioner's sugar (reserve 1 cup for rolling cookies)

2¼ cups flour

½ teaspoon salt

1 teaspoon vanilla

¼ cup pecans, finely chopped

1. Cream shortening and ½ cup confectioner's sugar. Add vanilla. Mix flour and salt, then stir into mixture.

2. Add pecans and mix well.

3. Shape dough into 1-inch balls; place on greased cookie sheet and bake at 375° for 12 minutes.

4. Roll hot cookies in remaining confectioner's sugar. Reroll cookies after they are cool, if desired.

CRUNCHY DATE BALLS

1 stick corn oil margarine

1 cup sugar

1 tablespoon water

8 ounces chopped dates

2 cups Rice Krispies

½ cup pecans or English walnuts, chopped

1 teaspoon vanilla

coconut or powdered sugar

1. Mix softened margarine, sugar, water, and dates in saucepan and bring to a boil. Cook 8 minutes, stirring constantly.

2. Remove from heat. Add Rice Krispies, nuts, and vanilla.

3. Shape into 1-inch balls and roll in coconut or powdered sugar.

4. Store in refrigerator in airtight container until ready to serve.

SHORTBREAD

¾ cups sugar

1½ cups butter

4 cups flour

1. Cream sugar and butter, then slowly add flour, mixing as you go.

2. Roll dough into 1½-inch balls and place on greased, nonstick cookie sheet. Press each ball with a detailed shortbread cookie press until about ½-inch thick.

3. Bake at 325° until just done. Don't brown or overbake.

Food in families is a sort of journal kept through the years. My children's children will not have known Clela, but I love that this tall sprite of a woman who came to love God during the time my parents pastored in the tiny farm community of Burlington, Michigan, will touch their lives in tangible ways, like these oatmeal cookies—the best and first cookies I ever learned to make. And maybe some of her delight in life, and her exuberant and sometimes reckless love for God, will touch them too, because her enthusiasm so affected their grandmother.

I've added applesauce to her recipe. Maybe my daughters or son will add some ingredient they discover; and as we all sit around the fire on cold winter days after school,

FOOD IN FAMILIES IS A SORT OF JOURNAL KEPT THROUGH THE YEARS.

having had fresh-from-the-oven oatmeal cookies and milk, we'll tell the stories that tie us all to a bigger story, and the love of God will become so real to those kids they can taste it. ❋

CLELA'S
OATMEAL COOKIES

1 cup soft shortening

1 cup white sugar

1 cup brown sugar

2 eggs

1 teaspoon vanilla

2 cups flour

1 teaspoon each:
salt
baking soda
baking powder

1 individual cup-serving
applesauce or 1 large jar of
Junior baby food applesauce

1 cup raisins (optional)

3 cups rolled oats

1. In large mixing bowl, cream together shortening, sugars, eggs, and vanilla.

2. In another bowl, mix flour, salt, baking soda, and baking powder.

3. Slowly add dry mixture to egg, sugar, and shortening mixture. Mix well.

4. Add applesauce and raisins (if desired). With heavy spoon or by hand, mix in 3 cups rolled oats until well blended.

5. Drop balls of cookie dough onto greased cookie sheet. Bake for 10 minutes at 375°.

6. Cool and store in sealed plastic container to keep moist and chewy.

IVAN PARKER
Colonial Peanut Oatmeal Cookies

COLONIAL
PEANUT OATMEAL COOKIES

1 cup shortening

1 cup granulated sugar

1 cup light brown sugar

1 teaspoon vanilla

2 eggs

1½ cups sifted flour

1 teaspoon baking soda

3 cups rolled oats

½ pound salted Spanish peanuts

1. Cream shortening. Gradually add sugars, then vanilla and eggs, and beat well.

2. Sift flour and baking soda; add to mixture.

3. Add rolled oats and peanuts. Mix well.

4. Shape dough into small balls.

5. Bake on lightly greased cookie sheet for about 7 minutes at 425°.

WES HAMPTON
Three-Sugar Cookies

We have lots of fun making these. We cut out fun shapes to decorate, omitting the raw coarse sugar. Then we make royal icing in different colors and decorate once the cookies have cooled. The kids love it. (And so do Mommy and Daddy!) ❄

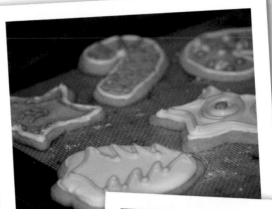

THREE-SUGAR COOKIES

3 cups all-purpose flour

1 teaspoon baking soda

¼ teaspoon salt

¼ cup light brown sugar, packed

1¾ cups white granulated sugar

2 sticks unsalted butter, room temperature

2 large eggs

1½ tablespoons pure vanilla extract

Raw coarse sugar (optional)

1. Preheat oven to 350°. Whisk together flour, baking soda, and salt, and set aside.

2. In a mixing bowl, combine brown sugar and white sugar, and mix on medium speed for 1 minute. Add butter and continue mixing until light and fluffy, scraping down sides of bowl halfway through. Add eggs, one at a time, mixing after each one. Add vanilla and mix until incorporated.

3. Gradually add in the flour mixture.

4. Roll dough into 1½- to 2-inch balls. Roll in the raw sugar until thoroughly coated (optional).

5. Flatten dough balls slightly with the palm of your hand and bake on a parchment-lined baking sheet or silicon mat for 13-18 minutes or until slightly browned.

6. Transfer to a wire cooling rack and allow to cool.

Wes's Three-Sugar Cookies are almost too beautiful to eat.

ROYAL ICING

There are several versions of Royal Icing. Some include lemon flavor; others exclude the lemon. Here is one recipe for Royal Icing. If you prefer a hint of lemon, add a few drops of lemon extract to the mixture after it thickens.

3 cups confectioner's sugar

¼ teaspoon cream of tartar

2 egg whites, beaten

1. In a bowl, sift together confectioner's sugar and cream of tartar.

2. Using electric mixer, beat in 2 beaten egg whites for about 5 minutes or until mixture is thick enough to hold its shape.

TORI TAFF
What's in a Cookie?

Many years ago, before Russ and I started our family, I began a tradition of making Christmas cookies to give as gifts. I used my mom's delicious butter cookie recipe, and I would spend one whole day baking the cookies and another whole day decorating them. I meticulously painted on the icing and then jazzed them up with every kind of sugary decoration you can imagine. They became known as Tori's Almost-Famous, Way-Too-Labor-Intensive Christmas Cookies—and even though I pretended to complain about what an effort they were to produce every year, I secretly LOVED all the compliments I received!

When Madi and Charlotte came along, I dreamily pictured the three of us continuing the tradition together, side-by-side in the kitchen—perhaps wearing adorable matching aprons—making the kinds of memories that would last a lifetime. When they were old enough to start asking if they could decorate cookies too, I happily made an extra dozen or so just for them. "Quantity rather than quality" best describes their decorating technique, as great gobs of frosting and piled-on jimmies and sprinkles were applied so lavishly that it was often hard to make out the shape of the cookie.

...I WOULD SPEND ONE WHOLE DAY BAKING THE COOKIES AND ANOTHER WHOLE DAY DECORATING THEM.

After the girls had thoroughly trashed the kitchen and eaten enough icing to put themselves into a sugar coma, they'd carefully place their creations on a special plate and cover it with foil. After tucking them into bed, I'd trudge downstairs to finish my cookies, staying up until the wee hours, doggedly determined to turn out another batch of beautiful gifts for all my friends to *ooh* and *aah* over.

One year when Madi was about eight, she asked if she could help me decorate the "real" cookies. "I'll do a very good job," she earnestly promised me. "Just give me a chance." I carefully explained that I would certainly make a batch of cookies just for her to decorate, but that only Mommy could really work on the ones that we gave away because they needed to be just so and it took a grown-up to do that. Her little face fell, and as she turned to leave the kitchen, she said sorrowfully, "This isn't really a very fun tradition if you're a kid." *Ouch.*

So, the next year I repented of my pride and put my quest for world cookie domination aside as I plastered on a smile and enthusiastically invited the girls to decorate with me. I bit my tongue as Charlotte clumped instead of sprinkled, and I turned my head when Madi combined frosting colors that clashed instead of complemented. The girls, of course, had a ball. More cookies were eaten than finished, and eventually they lost interest and drifted out of the kitchen, finally leaving me alone to painstakingly produce my miniature works of art. I'm happy to report that peace reigned, the spirit of Christmas prevailed...and thankfully, the girls didn't even notice that their cookies never quite made it to the holiday parties!

Tori Taff is a meticulous artist at work as she decorates her incredible cookie masterpieces, which she often gives away to friends.

I'd love to turn this story into a morality tale of how I learned to embrace life's little imperfections, and I'd love to leave you with the heartwarming image of my girls' sweet, raggedy cookies alongside my fancy ones on a festive gift plate—but I'm pretty sure it's a sin to tell a big fat lie at Christmastime. So instead, I'll reluctantly admit that though the Taff family does indeed have many cherished traditions we've created over the years, decorating cookies in matching aprons is not one of them.

As the girls got older, I realized (much to my relief) that the annual cookie marathon doesn't hold nearly as much fascination for teenagers as it did when they were small. It's too much work; they'd much rather eat them than decorate them. Russ likes to get in on that too. He could care less what his cookies look like, and he's also a big fan of the Heavy-Handed School of Icing approach. But every year I still wear myself out making trays of cookies so my friends can gush over them and I can modestly brush aside their praise. And every year the girls decorate a dozen or so just for their own enjoyment—sometimes they even give them as gifts to their own friends.

I guess if anyone has learned a life lesson out of this whole

Taste AND See
~ *Calvin Miller* ~

Give Grandma
a pail of berries
and watch her create a holy Nativity in the
richness of her gifts.
Jesus' mercy inhabits the common things
as well as the grand.
Christmas! The adoration of all things
great and small,
a celebration of the senses.

❧

The psalmist wrote, "O taste and see
that the Lord is good."
The goodness of the Lord is never clearer
than when we sit down to Christmas dinner.
And in the delight of the season,
our mouths water so furiously
that we can hardly say grace—
our best prayer effort
used up in the waiting.
The children take the abbreviated
way to table grace:

God is great
God is good
Let us thank Him
For our food.

Yet we are not so much in a hurry
that we do not remember there are others
less fortunate than we are.

Continued on page 150

thing, it's probably Madi Rose and Charlotte. Maybe growing up with a crazed, cookie-making perfectionist for a mother taught them a little something about tolerance, patience, and forgiving one another's faults. My fondest Christmas wish for them is that someday they'll have sweet daughters of their own, and they can lovingly carry on our untraditional family tradition by shooing them out of the kitchen too! ❄

TORI'S ALMOST-FAMOUS, WAY-TOO-LABOR-INTENSIVE CHRISTMAS COOKIES

1¾ cups flour

½ teaspoon baking powder

2/3 cup butter, softened

½ cup sugar

1 egg, beaten

½ to 1 teaspoon vanilla

½ to 1 teaspoon almond extract

1. Mix flour and baking powder together.

2. Cream butter; add sugar until well blended.

3. Mix in egg; add vanilla and almond flavoring.

4. Add the dry ingredients in two or three portions, blending together until smooth.

5. Chill dough in refrigerator.

6. Roll out dough to medium width—not too thick, not too thin—and cut out with cookie cutters.

7. Bake at 375° for 6-8 minutes, checking often.

8. I usually double or even triple this recipe. I make Royal Icing with meringue powder to use as my base icing—dividing it among several styrofoam cups and using food coloring to create lots of different colors. I use buttercream decorating icing to add flowers, leaves, lines, and textures. Add jimmies, sprinkles, colored sugar, nonpareils, luster dust, sugar pearls, etc., while frosting is still slightly moist.

Landon Ritchie is pleased with the freshly decorated cookies he and his family made as part of their Christmas Eve tradition.

CHARLOTTE RITCHIE
Christmas Eve's Delicious Traditions

When Greg and I married, we wanted to incorporate the Christmas traditions of our families but also start our own. Every Christmas Eve we bake cookies together. Landon's favorite are sugar cookies because he likes the different shapes and he loves decorating them.

In the evening we eat dinner—usually some kind of soup or chili. Greg's chili is amazing! Then we go look at Christmas lights. Our favorite place is in Georgia. It's a display called "Lights of the South." The location is a huge farm that is transformed into a Christmas wonderland. You start by taking a hay ride through the woods. There are lights and decorations of every kind everywhere. Next, you can drink hot chocolate or apple cider while roasting marshmallows over an open fire. At the end, they have a small cottage where Santa waits to speak to and take pictures with the children. It's such a fun experience!

We then go home and open one gift, which is always new pajamas for everyone. Then we set out cookies and milk for Santa and read the Christmas story. It's a tradition that really brings our family together. ❄

CONNIE HOPPER
Chocolate Balls

CHOCOLATE BALLS

2½ cups graham cracker crumbs

1 pound confectioner's sugar

2 sticks butter, melted

2 (3-ounce) cans flaked coconut (or 2 cups raisins, or 1 can/cup of each)

1 (12-ounce) jar crunchy peanut butter

1 cup nuts, chopped

5-6 squares semi-sweet chocolate (or more as needed), melted

1. Add sugar to graham cracker crumbs. Blend in butter. Add coconut and raisins, peanut butter, and nuts. Blend well using hands.

2. Shape into tightly packed balls and dip into melted chocolate. Place on wax paper to harden.

Taste AND *See*
~ *Calvin Miller* ~

Christmas is that time of year when,
as the charitable collectors said to Ebenezer,
"Want is keenly felt and abundance rejoices."
Abundance,
abundance, abundance!
Jesus was never stingy!
He fed the five thousand so abundantly
that there were twelve baskets of leftovers.
All this from that great Messiah who said,
"I have come that they might have life,
and have it more abundantly."

Christ is the founder of every worthy feast,
and perhaps we should remember the
wisdom of Tiny Tim.
He said he was crippled and
he hoped people would see him in church,
for it might be pleasant for them to
remember on Christmas day
who made lame beggars walk and blind men see.
It is a reasonable remembrance.
Jesus really is the reason for the season.
And Jesus is the Lord of abundance.
And Christmas Day is a day to eat our fill
and remember Him whose final banquet,
the Wedding Supper of the Lamb,
is still to come.

Continued on page 154

JEFF & SHERI EASTER
Double Delicious Cookie Bars

DOUBLE DELICIOUS COOKIE BARS

½ cup butter

1½ cups graham cracker crumbs

1 (14-ounce) can Eagle Brand® milk

1 (12-ounce) package Hershey® chocolate chips

1 cup Reese's® peanut butter chips

1. Melt butter and pour over graham cracker crumbs. Press into a baking dish.

2. Pour Eagle Brand® milk over crumb mixture.

3. Top with chocolate chips and peanut butter chips.

4. Bake at 350° for 25-30 minutes.

5. Cool and cut into bars.

Sheri Easter and her girls dig in to their Double Delicious Cookie Bars before Jeff and Madison get to them.

KAREN PECK-GOOCH
Our Family Favorite

My friend Ronda gave me this wonderful recipe several years ago. My daughter Kari and I especially love baking these cookies during the holidays. This is my family's favorite cookie. ❄

Ronda's Bits 'O Brickle Cookies

6 ounces Heath® Bits 'O Brickle toffee

1½ tablespoons liquid shortening

6 tablespoons self-rising flour

½ cup butter

6 tablespoons sugar

6 tablespoons brown sugar

½ teaspoon vanilla flavoring

1 egg

1¼ cups plus 2 tablespoons self-rising flour

1. Preheat oven to 325°.

2. Mix together toffee, liquid shortening, and flour, and set aside.

3. In large bowl, combine butter, sugar, brown sugar, and vanilla. Beat until creamy.

4. Add egg. Gradually add flour.

5. Mix well, then stir in coated Bits 'O Brickle.

6. Drop by teaspoons onto greased cookie sheet.

7. Bake for 10-12 minutes.

Judy Nelon
Rex's Favorite Christmas Cookies

It was Christmas the first time Rex invited me to meet his family in his hometown of Asheville, North Carolina. We were both shy and quiet as we drove up the mountain to the place where he had lived until he moved to Atlanta to join his first full-time quartet: the LeFevres.

As we traveled up the steep, winding road, this usually shy man began to honk his horn to alert everyone that he was back home for Christmas. It was here in the Blue Ridge Mountains that Rex was born. Here is where he began singing bass after his voice lowered from the tenor he had originally been. The area he was from was known as Spook Mountain, and he told me it had been scary for him to walk those dark roads late at night as a boy. It calmed him to sing loudly as he walked back home after his singing lessons in town.

Many friends recalled their Rex Nelon stories to me that day. Rex bragged about and looked forward to his mom, Marietta Nelon, making all his favorite dishes even though she was now eighty-nine years of age. Later in the day, he loaded us all up to ride around the mountain. Suddenly Rex pulled the car over in front of a house and bolted up to the door alone. He went into this house without even knocking.

Rex's mother smiled: "We probably won't be here long. Rex has just gone in to get his favorite cookies that Mrs. Knighten has baked for him all his life." And sure enough, in just a matter of minutes, he was back in the car with his tin of cookies under his arm. He reluctantly opened the top and offered me one, warning, "And I mean just one. These are mine!"

I learned that day that Mrs. Knighten's cookies had

Judy Nelon learned something new about Rex's love for a certain Christmas cookie during their first Christmas together.

been his favorite thing in the world to eat. Later I asked Mildred Knighten if she would mind sharing this special recipe with me. She was happy to, and now I would like to share it with you. Along with Rex's mother's cooking, it was something he looked forward to experiencing again each Christmas in Asheville. ❄

JIM BRADY
Snowball Cookies

One of my favorite holiday memories is when we kids would help my mom decorate the Christmas cookies each year. My job was putting on the sprinkles, and in my little-boy mind, it was an important job indeed! Having the right ratio of sprinkles to cookie was very important!

Now that Melissa and I are making Christmas traditions of our own, I look forward to her famous Snowball Cookies. They're covered in powdered sugar, and she makes them bite-sized, so you can just pop the whole thing right in your mouth! If there are any left after Christmas, they usually become breakfast. The next morning, we'll put on a pot of coffee and finish them off. Yum! ❄

REX NELON'S FAVORITE DATE NUT COOKIES

1 (40-count) package dates

1 cup water

1 cup sugar

½ teaspoon baking soda

½ teaspoon salt

1 cup brown sugar

1½ cups rolled oats, uncooked

½ pound butter, melted

½ cup pecans, chopped

1. Cut dates into pieces and cook with water and sugar until thick. Set aside to cool.

2. Combine dry ingredients, oats, and melted butter, then mix until crumbly. Add nuts.

3. Layer crumbs in a 13 x 9 pan, reserving 1/3 of mixture for topping. (Mildred's husband, Gordon, says the secret is their fifty-year-old pan.) Finish top with remaining mixture.

4. Bake at 325° for 30-35 minutes. Cut into squares.

Jim Brady demonstrates the perfect pop-in-your-mouth goodness of his wife's bite-sized Snowball Cookies.

SNOWBALL COOKIES

½ cup powdered sugar

1 cup butter, softened

2 teaspoons vanilla

2 cups self-rising flour

1. Preheat oven to 325°.

2. In a large bowl, combine sugar, butter, and vanilla, and blend well.

3. Stir in flour until dough holds together. Shape into 1-inch balls.

4. Place 1 inch apart on ungreased cookie sheet.

5. Bake for 15 to 20 minutes or until set but not brown. Immediately remove from cookie sheet.

6. Cool slightly; roll in powdered sugar.

7. Cool completely; roll again in powdered sugar.

ANN DOWNING
Easy Crunch Bars

I love the combination of salty and sweet. This is one of the best recipes for that. Of course, chocolate is one of those "cravings" I have . . . and Christmas is no different. ❈

EASY CRUNCH BARS

35 saltine or club crackers

½ cup butter or margarine

½ cup firmly packed light brown sugar

1 cup white chocolate chips

1. Preheat oven to 400°.

2. Place crackers in foil-lined 15 x 10 x 1 baking pan.

3. Place butter and brown sugar in saucepan, cook on medium-high heat until butter is completely melted and mixture is well blended, stirring occasionally.

4. Bring to a boil. Boil for 3 minutes without stirring. Then spread over crackers.

5. Bake 5-7 minutes or until topping is golden brown. Immediately sprinkle with chopped chocolate, then let stand for 5 minutes or until chocolate is softened.

6. Spread chocolate evenly over ingredients in pan. Cool. Break into pieces.

LUANN BURGER
Italian Pizzelles

These traditional waffle cookies have been a Christmas favorite for many generations in our family.

ITALIAN PIZZELLES

½ cup butter

⅔ cup sugar

3 eggs

1¾ to 2 cups all-purpose flour

1 teaspoon baking powder

1 teaspoon vanilla
(anise or lemon flavoring may be substituted)

pinch of salt

These traditional waffle cookies have been a Christmas favorite for many generations in Luann Burger's family.

Taste AND *See*
~ *Calvin Miller* ~

Christmas is our high day of obligation.

A day when we, the fortunate,

must set the table of the less fortunate.

For it is the Christ of Christmas who

teaches us all:

"Compassion is the best way

to remember the season of My birth.

Taste and see that I, your Lord, am good.

Eat, drink and be thoughtful."

So, let us truly sense Christmas—smelling it,

listening to it, touching it, seeing it, tasting it.

Then, sensing the wonder of it all,

let us agree warmly with the little Cratchit boy:

"God bless us . . . everyone."

Fruitcake

1. Preheat the pizzelle maker according to the manufacturer's instructions.

2. Mix all ingredients together into a soft-textured batter.

3. Place a heaping tablespoon of batter onto the center of the pizzelle maker grid and close the lid. Within 15 seconds, your first pizzelle should be lightly browned. Remove carefully with a fork and cool flat on parchment paper or a brown paper bag. Continue until all the batter is used.

4. Once cooled, sprinkle pizzelles generously with powdered sugar. (They can be frozen for up to three months without the powdered sugar.)

KEVIN WILLIAMS
An Ode to the Fruitcake

Well, the holidays are here again. My favorite time of the year. Time for family, fellowship, and lots of food.

Every family has its own traditions and recipes for memorable meals, so I would like to take a few moments and explore the concept of the Christmas fruitcake. From what country did this yuletide delicacy originate? Who was the first person to say: "Hey, let's take some flour, sugar, maraschino cherries, walnuts, pineapple, dates, and a whole bunch of raisins, and make a really heavy cake out of it, then pass it on to everyone we call our friends, so they can pass it on too. And what if we teach our children how to make it so they can perpetuate this holiday tragedy with their offspring for generations to come?"

Johnny Carson's theory was that there has only been one fruitcake ever made. It's been sent from person to person for decades, even centuries. Jerry Seinfeld called it "regifting." I call it "making memories."

To whom would you send your signature fruitcake? I have a few suggestions. Let's start with your creditors. Why not send the mortgage company a brick-sized piece of holiday love with a note that says, "I know my payments haven't been exactly on time lately, so here's something for you to chew on"? What about the kid on his bike who throws your newspaper in the neighbor's yard day after day? Greet him with your own blend of congealed magic to say, "Thanks, hope you can haul it home." Perhaps the best recipient would be your mother-in-law. Just give it to her in front of everyone and tell her the kids made it especially for her. Tell her it's a holiday jalapeno cake and watch the excitement begin. Let me know how it goes. ❄

Keeping your favorite
ingredients handy in festive
containers like Lori Phelps
has done here is a simple
way to make holiday baking
extra fun and convenient.

Lipton

GLORIA GAITHER
*Fruitcake That
People Actually Love . . .*

There is nothing more nostalgic or traditional at Christmas than fruitcake or plum pudding. Trouble is, most people don't really like fruitcake. They say it's dry, or it's too bitter with citrus. I kept experimenting with ingredients and various combinations from recipes until I came upon this incredibly moist, delicious, and beautiful fruitcake. For starters, there isn't much cake—it's all fruit (no citrus), nuts, and yummy goo. And, to top that off, it's soaked with an elixir that only makes the ingredients grow more flavorful when kept wrapped in the refrigerator for two weeks or more. So I make fruitcake early in December, before things get too hectic, and when dear friends drop by unexpectedly or I run into my beautician, Bill's barber, or the UPS man (who are all old friends by now too), I have something to give that is from our own kitchen, yet fit for the most elegant party.

Of course, I have to hide these cakes in the refrigerator behind the loaves of wheat bread, cartons of brown eggs, and bags of fresh produce and grapes. If I don't, Bill finds them in the night and whittles away at them "just a sliver" at a time. So I keep a couple where he can find them and bury the rest behind things.

NECTAR-SOAKED FRUITCAKE
CAKE RECIPE

2 eggs, lightly beaten

*1 (28-oz.) jar canned Borden's®
None Such Mincemeat with Brandy*

*1 ⅓ cups (or 15-ounce can) sweetened condensed
milk (like Eagle Brand®)*

1 cup candied red cherries

½ cup candied green cherries

½ cup candied pineapple chunks

1 cup walnuts or pecans, broken

2½ cups flour

1 teaspoon baking soda

1. Grease and dust one 9-inch tube pan, two regular-sized bread pans, or four small loaf pans with some flour.

2. Combine eggs, mincemeat, sweetened condensed milk, fruit, and nuts.

3. Fold in dry ingredients.

4. Divide into pans.

5. Garnish top(s) of cake(s) with half-slices of candied pineapple, whole red and green candied cherries, and walnuts or pecans.

6. Bake at 300° for 2 hours if using tube pan, about 1 hour for large bread pans, and about 40 minutes for smaller loaf pans. Check center with a baking test stick. When stick comes out without wet dough, remove from oven.

NECTAR RECIPE

2 cups apricot nectar

¾ cup white Karo® syrup

¼ cup rum or brandy (if desired)

1. While cakes are baking, heat apricot nectar and Karo syrup in a saucepan until just ready to boil. Add rum or brandy and turn off heat and cover.

2. When cakes are done, poke holes in cakes using a meat fork, and spoon nectar over cakes, allowing the liquid to soak in. Continue until cakes have absorbed liquid and surfaces are glazed.

3. Let cakes cool in pans.

4. When cool, turn each cake upside-down on heavy plastic wrap; wrap and seal. Then wrap in foil and store in refrigerator for up to three weeks.

For giving as a gift, tie with Christmas ribbon and tag with handmade greetings. To enjoy at home, just slice and serve with tea or coffee. ❊

Beyond Christmas
AN AFTERWORD

❄ ❄ ❄

*Now we see things imperfectly
as in a cloudy mirror, but then we will see
everything with perfect clarity.
All that I know now is partial and incomplete,
but then I will know everything completely,
just as God now knows me completely.*

1 CORINTHIANS 13:12 NLT

THE LETDOWN:
When Christmas Is Over

EMILY SUTHERLAND

For many of us, Christmas is followed by a strange sadness—the "letdown"—after all the anticipation and celebrating.

We can't help it. We are humans living in an imperfect and ever-changing world. We have baggage, and expectations, and sin that reminds us every single day—especially at Christmas—that even this world's most wonderful experiences will never live up to the wonderful World for which we were made.

The good news of Jesus is, our redemption didn't just buy our forgiveness for all the shortcomings that are bound into our nature here on earth. Thirty-three years after that Bethlehem baby was laid in a prickly manger of hay, He purchased with His very life a Home for us where the celebration is perfect—where the music and the feast and the relationships and the atmosphere and the unsurpassed beauty are everything we have ever longed for. At last, we will no longer be trying to recreate something too eternal for our senses to contain. We will be living in the midst of it all!

Perfection is a myth here on earth. We will never have a perfect Christmas, a perfect family, a perfect experience. Our greenery will dry out and make a mess; our poinsettias will die. Those mouth-watering treats will all be consumed, after which we will likely gain a few pounds. And we will most likely give and receive some wrong gifts now and then—gifts that may be returned for something else. But don't let any of those small disappointments rob you of the joy that was born for you at Christmas. Rather, let them point you to that day of all days when we will finally celebrate our first perfect Christmas.

For now, it is worth every ounce of energy we have to bring honor to this holy story with our very best offerings. As we attempt to communicate the greatest story ever told, it takes all five of our human senses to begin to grasp even a piece of it. Yet even then, we need the touch of our Savior, who gave His last ounce of life for us.

He longs to celebrate with us—to hear us sing and tell His Story.

He delights in seeing the beauty that we create for His birthday.

He takes joy in our personal incense offerings, whatever they may be,

and sits at our feast as we share His abundance.

And perhaps best of all, He delights to embrace us with His holy presence! ❅

Listen to your life.
See it for the fathomless mystery it is.
In the boredom and pain of it no less than in the excitement and gladness:
touch, taste, smell your way to the holy and hidden heart of it
because in the last analysis
all moments are key moments,
and life itself is grace.

FREDERICK BUECHNER FROM *NOW AND THEN*

HOPE

BILL GAITHER

I was probably five years old on the Christmas Eve when we got word that my cousin Glen had been killed in World War II. He was a young, fun-loving guy, and to think of him in a war across the ocean in a foreign place at Christmas was difficult to imagine. Even more difficult was knowing that he would never come home for another family Christmas. Hearing that news was, for me, a moment of profound sadness that remains an undercurrent to the joys of Christmas seventy years later.

However, I know something now that I didn't fully realize when I was five. Though sadness is a part of life on this side of eternity—maybe especially at Christmas (as well as many of our other days throughout the year)—*Hope* is greater. Hope is not fragile; it infuses every joy and pain with the eternal promise of Christmas: "I came that you might have Life, and have it more abundantly." ❊

"Christmas is a time when you get homesick—even when you're home."

CAROL NELSON

PHOTO CREDITS

❧

Photos from iStockPhoto ©2011,
used by permission, appear on pages:

37 (Footbridge, Nashville, TN)

38 (Cardinal)

40 (Candle)

41 (Mall)

45 (Snowflakes)

46 (Victorian carolers, 1864)

48 (Snowflakes)

54 (Nativity)

61 (Christmas tree, NYC)

62 (Manger)

71 (Snowy river)

78 (Gun)

78 (Figure skates)

88 (City carriage)

93 (Winter scene)

98 (Snowy pines)

99 (Sawed pine)

100 (Sand volleyball)

113 (Pine branch)

113 (Snowy fence)

116 (Hot breakfast)

120 (Orange)

132 (Éclair)

136 (Ornaments)

143 (Star cookies)

144 (Oatmeal cookies)

148 (Decorated cookies)

153 (Snowball pastries)

155 (Fruitcake)

161 (Winter scene)

❧

Photos from BigStock ©2011,
used by permission, appear on pages:

35 (Snowy street, NYC)

108 (Baby in manger)

ADDITIONAL PHOTOGRAPHY

❧

MELODY GAITHER
1, 18, 42, 74, 82, 110, 124 (Bill and Gloria's grandson, Liam)

GLORIA GAITHER
20 (Bill and Gloria's front porch decorated for Christmas)

ERIC SCOTT
21 (White Christmas tree at Gaither Family Resources)

MATT MULLER
31 (Reba Rambo-McGuire peppermint tree)

EMILY SUTHERLAND
45, 53, 72 (Hymn books)
58 (Guitar)
77 (Popcorn strands)
92 (Sparkling snow)
103 (Anti-itch lotion and thermometer)
112 (Ice-covered evergreen)
115 (Potpourri)
121 (Candlelight)
126 (Jelly jars)
133 (Wassail)
135 (Peanut butter fudge)
137 ("Happy Birthday, Jesus" cake)
139 (Bell cookie cutter)

JACKSON SUTHERLAND
76 (Stringing popcorn)
77 (Crafts-in-the-making)
119 (Teaberry gum)
122 (Oranges and cloves)

TERI GARNER AND ERIC SCOTT
64 (Bells and pine)

LORI PHELPS
96 (Roaring fire)
105 (Basket of books, "For unto Us" plaque)
158–159 (Wrought-iron window with curtain)

STEPHEN TORRENCE
29, 50, 59, 121 (Buddy Greene headshots)

All used by permission.

Bill and Gloria Gaither

Bill and Gloria Gaither's records and Homecoming videos have sold over 100 million copies. More importantly, together they have deeply impacted the kingdom of God with the hundreds of hymns and gospel standards they've penned such as "He Touched Me," "Something Beautiful" and "There's Just Something about That Name." Each year the Gaithers and their Homecoming friends perform before hundreds of thousands at their arena events, festivals and cruises. Gloria has authored more than 40 books, including *Let's Make a Memory*, which has sold over 400,000 copies.

IF YOU LIKED THIS BOOK . . .

- Tell your friends by going to: http://www.ahomecomingchristmas.com and clicking "LIKE"

- Share the video book trailer by posting it on your Facebook page

- Head over to our Facebook page, click "LIKE" and post a comment regarding what you enjoyed about the book

- Tweet "I recommend reading #AHomecomingChristmas by @Gaithermusic"

- Hashtag: #AHomecomingChristmas

- Subscribe to our newsletter by going to http://worthypublishing.com/about/subscribe.php

WORTHY PUBLISHING
FACEBOOK PAGE

WORTHY PUBLISHING
WEBSITE